Dartmoor

WALKS

Originally compiled by
Brian Conduit,
John Brooks
and Sue Viccars
Fully revised by
Sue Viccars

JARROLD
publishing

D0240951

Acknowledgements

We would like to thank Mr P.W. Broomhead, Regional Director of the National Trust, for looking at the original manuscript and giving much useful advice. We are also grateful to the Dartmoor National Park Authority for their help.

Text:	Brian Conduit, John Brooks, Sue Viccars
	Revised text for 2007 edition, Sue Viccars
Photography:	Brian Conduit, John Brooks
Editorial:	Ark Creative (UK) Ltd.
Design:	Ark Creative (UK) Ltd.
Series Consultant:	Brian Conduit

Jarrold Publishing   ISBN 978-0-7117-0515-9

While every care has been taken to ensure the accuracy of the route directions, the publishers cannot accept responsibility for errors or omissions, or for changes in details given. The countryside is not static: hedges and fences can be removed, field boundaries can alter, footpaths can be rerouted and changes in ownership can result in the closure or diversion of some concessionary paths. Also, paths that are easy and pleasant for walking in fine conditions may become slippery, muddy and difficult in wet weather, while stepping stones across rivers and streams may become impassable.

If you find an inaccuracy in either the text or maps, please write or e-mail to Jarrold Publishing at the addresses below.

First published 1989
by Jarrold Publishing and Ordnance Survey
Revised and reprinted 1990, 1991, 1994, 1996, 1997, 2002, 2004, 2007.

Printed in Singapore. 9/07

Jarrold Publishing
Pathfinder Guides, Healey House, Dene Road, Andover, Hampshire SP10 2AA
e-mail: info@totalwalking.co.uk
www.totalwalking.co.uk

Front cover: Bowerman's Nose – a Dartmoor landmark
Previous page: An inviting footpath near Moretonhampstead

Contents

The National Trust; The Ramblers' Association; Walkers and the Law; Countryside Access Charter; Global Positioning System (GPS); Safety on the Hills: Useful Organisations; Ordnance Survey Maps

Short, easy walks

Walks of modest length, likely to involve some modest uphill walking

More challenging walks which may be longer and/or over more rugged terrain, often with some stiff climbs

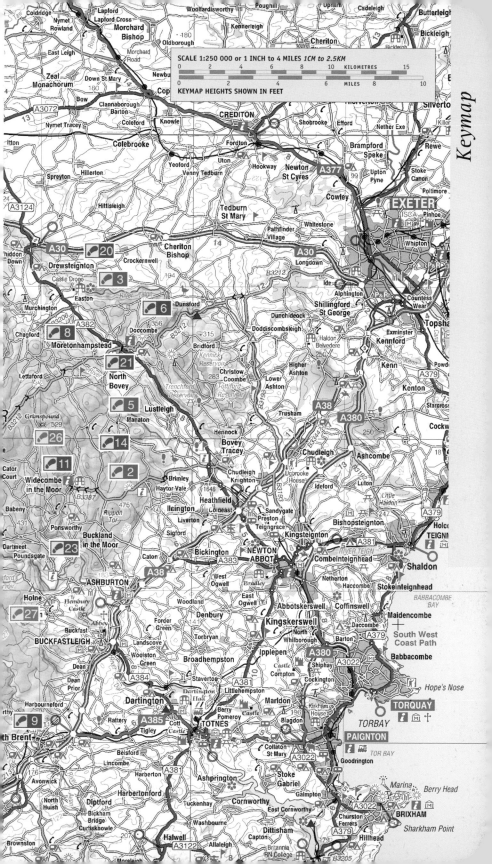

At-a-glance...

Walk	Page	Start	Nat. Grid Reference	Distance	Time	Highest Point
Burrator reservoir and Sheeps Tor	28	Burrator reservoir	SX 569693	5½ miles (8.9km)	3 hrs	785ft (240m)
Castle Drogo and Teign Gorge	18	Fingle Bridge	SX 743899	4 miles (6.4km)	2 hrs	820ft (250m)
Chagford and the River Teign	30	Chagford	SX 702874	4 miles (6.4km)	2 hrs	1050ft (320m)
Dartmeet, Combestone and Brimpts Wood	38	Dartmeet	SX 672732	6½ miles (10.5km)	3½ hrs	1150ft (350m)
Drewsteignton, Hittisleigh Barton and Crockernwell	60	Drewsteignton	SX 735908	8 miles (12.9km)	4 hrs	720ft (220m)
Gidleigh, Kes Tor and Teign-e-ver Bridge	48	Frenchbeer Rock	SX 672853	5½ miles (8.9km)	3 hrs	1380ft (420m)
Grimspound, Coombe Down and Challacombe	78	Bennett's Cross, near Postbridge	SX 679815	9½ miles (15.3km)	5½ hrs	1590ft (485m)
Haytor	16	Haytor	SX 759767	3½ miles (5.6km)	2 hrs	1410ft (430m)
Holne Moor and Snowdon	82	Holne	SX 706694	9 miles (14.5km)	4½ hrs	1690ft (515m)
Horrabridge and Sampford Spiney	46	Horrabridge	SX 513699	6 miles (9.7km)	3 hrs	820ft (250m)
Ivybridge, the Erme valley and Western Beacon	40	Ivybridge	SX 635566	7½ miles (12.1km)	4 hrs	1095ft (334m)
Lustleigh Cleave	22	Lustleigh	SX 784812	5 miles (8km)	2½ hrs	1050ft (320m)
Lydford Gorge	14	Lydford	SX 510847	3½ miles (5.6km)	2 hrs	210ft (64m)
Manaton, Hound Tor and Becka Falls	43	Manaton	SX 749811	7 miles (11.3km)	4 hrs	1280ft (390m)
Mary Tavy, Horndon Down and Peter Tavy	66	Mary Tavy	SX 508787	7 miles (11.3km)	4 hrs	1085ft (330m)
Moretonhampstead, Butterdon Down and N. Bovey	63	Moretonhampstead	SX 753860	8½ miles (13.7km)	4½ hrs	1085ft (330m)
New Bridge and Dr Blackall's Drive	69	New Bridge	SX 711708	6 miles (9.7km)	3 hrs	1150ft (350m)
Okehampton, Cullever Steps and Belstone	50	Okehampton	SX 587951	7½ miles (12.1km)	4½ hrs	1540ft (470m)
Plym Woods and Wigford Down	20	Shaugh Bridge	SX 533636	4 miles (6.4km)	2 hrs	820ft (250m)
Postbridge, Laughter Hole and Belstone	57	Postbridge	SX 647788	7½ miles (12.1km)	4 hrs	1180ft (360m)
Princetown, Whiteworks and Crock of Gold	72	Princetown	SX 590734	7½ miles (12.1km)	3½ hrs	1475ft (450m)
Ringmoor Down, Eylesbarrow and Siward's Cross	86	Near Ringmoor Cottage	SX 559669	9 miles (14.5km)	5 hrs	1475ft (450m)
South Brent and the Avon valley	32	South Brent	SX 698602	5½ miles (8.9km)	3 hrs	1017ft (310m)
South Zeal and Little Hound Tor	54	South Zeal	SX 648932	6 miles (9.7km)	3½ hrs	1540ft (470m)
Steps Bridge and Mardon Down	25	Steps Bridge	SX 803883	7½ miles (12.1km)	3½ hrs	1115ft (340m)
Two Bridges, Wistman's Wood and the West Dart	75	Two Bridges	SX 609750	9 miles (14.5km)	6 hrs	1663ft (507m)
Walkham valley and Merrivale	34	Merrivale	SX 553750	5½ miles (8.9km)	2½ hrs	1215ft (370m)
Widecombe in the Moor and Hamel Down	36	Widecombe in the Moor	SX 719768	7 miles (11.3km)	3½ hrs	1745ft (532m)

Comments

The energetic part of this walk comes at the start with the ascent of Sheeps Tor, one of Dartmoor's finest viewpoints. The return is by the tree-lined shores of the reservoir, a famous beauty spot.

Much of the route is either above or through the thickly wooded Teign Gorge, with a chance to visit a 20th-century castle.

Apart from the initial climb out of delightful Chagford, there are few gradients on this stroll, which mixes a riverside section of the Two Moors Way with paths through woodland and over moor.

Be warned before you start this walk that the river crossings may be dangerous after heavy rain. If conditions are favourable you will find yourself walking through some of Dartmoor's finest scenery.

This takes the walker away from the moors and valleys and into the countryside of mid Devon. The small fields and tall hedges give the feeling of another era.

The opening part of the walk takes you across bare and lonely moorland, while the return, following the Two Moors Way, goes through woods and fields. It makes an excellent excursion.

There is a grand mix here of walking on the high moor, through woodland and over fields. Furthermore, the walk takes you to Grimspound, the most impressive of Dartmoor's prehistoric settlements.

Fine views and relics of Dartmoor's industrial heritage are enjoyed on this walk, which is dominated by the imposing presence of Haytor.

A clear day and a compass are vital for this expedition, which covers moorland often without an obvious path. The lower parts of the walk are on country lanes and bridleways.

The route explores an isolated part of western Dartmoor where the gradients are easy and the countryside unspoilt. There are two lengths of road to walk but these carry little traffic.

This typical Dartmoor walk begins with a gentle climb up one of the grandest river valleys. Later, the walking becomes harder, and you must be confident of navigation in the final moorland section.

An outward route along the top edge of the Bovey valley is followed by a lower-level return, mainly through attractive woodland.

The walk takes you along both sides of a steep, narrow and thickly wooded ravine. Note that this route cannot be walked during the winter months.

Bird-watchers will find opportunities for seeing a wide range of species in the ancient woodland at the end of this route, though dedicated walkers may favour the earlier moorland sections.

Although only 7 miles (11.3km), the walk calls for an unexpected amount of stamina. In compensation it takes you to some delightful yet neglected countryside, once intensively mined.

This is a figure-of-eight route based on Moretonhampstead, which can be tackled in one or two parts. North Bovey is one of the loveliest of West Country villages.

An energetic route with superlative views, especially over the Dart gorge, and splendid riverside, woodland and moorland walking.

Apart from some wooded stretches beside the West and East Okement rivers at the beginning and end, this is Dartmoor at its wildest and most austere.

This walk in the Plym valley includes fine woodland, open downland, views over moor and coast and relics of Dartmoor's industrial history.

This is a walk particularly recommended for children as it offers constantly changing landscapes with a succession of streams to cross by ford or stepping stones.

The paths are level but may be moist on this route, which gives the bleak flavour of Dartmoor in *Hound of the Baskervilles*. Navigation should not provide any problems if you are good at map-reading.

This walk covers lonely moorland at the heart of the moor, and it is advisable to have a compass in case the clouds fall low. The archaeological treasures of Drizzle Combe are impressive even for Dartmoor.

Much of the first part of the route is across open moorland. This is followed by a walk through woodland above the Avon valley, starting and finishing with a delightful stretch by the river.

Some of Dartmoor's ancient monuments are situated in lonely locations – this walk into the northern moor takes you to a stone circle and 'The Graveyard', a mysterious stone row 447ft (136m) long.

In springtime Dunsford Wood is ablaze with hosts of daffodils, and the riverside section of the walk becomes crowded. However, you will seldom find many people on breezy Mardon Down.

This is another walk to avoid if there has been recent prolonged rain. It calls for little climbing but covers some wonderful scenery – Powder Mills is a lovely, haunted, spot.

There are fine views all the way, and at the end you can explore the Merrivale Antiquities, which are among the largest groups of prehistoric remains on Dartmoor.

Stamina is needed for the climb to the moor from Widecombe but after this the gradients are easy and the views superb. Children will enjoy opportunities for rock scrambles on the tors the route passes.

At-a-glance...

Introduction to Dartmoor

A short journey northwards from the coast of South Devon subjects you to one of the most abrupt changes of scenery likely to be encountered anywhere in the country. A few miles in distance and a few hundred feet in height, and you are transported from the lush, almost subtropical conditions on the coast (palm trees grow on the promenade at Torquay) to the open and majestic terrain of Dartmoor, thinly populated, sometimes bleak, and justifiably acclaimed as the last great wilderness in southern England.

The two major east–west roads from Exeter to Cornwall do not cross Dartmoor, but skirt it – the A30 along its northern and the A38 along its southern edge. Main roads across the moor are relatively few and side roads and country lanes here are often narrower than in other parts of the country, as many an exasperated holiday motorist venturing here for the first time on a day out from the nearby holiday resorts can testify. The lanes may be hardly more than rough farm tracks and, provided there is little or no traffic, make good walking routes. Likewise, although the moor is ringed with towns – Exeter (the chief gateway), Ashburton and Newton Abbot to the east, Okehampton to the north, Tavistock to the west and Plymouth, Totnes and the coastal resorts of Torbay to the south – there are few towns and villages on the moor itself. As for the villages, they are mostly concentrated around the edges, particularly in the river valleys and the gentler country on the eastern side; on the wilder expanses of the north and west they are largely non-existent.

Wide variety of scenery

Within Dartmoor itself there is a wide variety of scenery, the central heartland of the open moors being surrounded by pleasant river valleys with picture-postcard villages of thatch and granite, as well as by rolling downland and steep-sided, thickly wooded gorges. The valleys are benign and welcoming, the downs make fine viewpoints and the gorges are dramatic. The moors, in striking contrast, can be most inhospitable, even dangerous, and need to be treated with caution and respect. Route-finding across these bare expanses can be difficult, as paths that look easy to follow on a map are not always visible on the ground, and the lack of easily identifiable landmarks can lead to a walker getting lost, especially in misty conditions. Stories of escaped convicts arriving back at the prison gates after only a few hours' exposure to a Dartmoor mist, almost begging to be let in again, are no myth. But even in the wildest parts, these austere, sweeping moorlands, their hilltops studded with the ubiquitous granite tors that are the most characteristic element of the Dartmoor landscape, are endowed with a haunting and melancholic beauty. The scene may also be enhanced by the presence of the delightful and hardy Dartmoor ponies.

In general, the gentler scenery is to be found in the south and east and the wilder terrain in the north and west. Much of central Dartmoor is an uninhabited wilderness – almost free of villages, farms, trees and roads – of outstanding environmental value, functioning mainly as a stock-rearing and water-catchment area and as a military training ground. From this soggy mass rise Dartmoor's rivers – the Lyd, Tavy, Meavy, Walkham, Plym, Yealm, Erme, Avon, East and West Dart, Bovey, Teign, Taw and Okement – all of which except the last two flow southwards, eventually reaching the English Channel.

The reasons for the differences in scenery and also the flow of the rivers lie in the geology and weather. Dartmoor, along with Bodmin Moor and other smaller areas of Cornish moorland, is a great mass of granite rising above the surrounding farming country like a brooding giant. Immense primeval earth movements tilted this mass towards the south and east, which is why the highest (and wettest) land is in the north and west and why the majority of the rivers flow southwards. The granite core is edged with areas of softer rocks – slates, shales, limestone and sandstone – and where the rivers leave the harder granite and reach these softer rocks they have sometimes cut deep, narrow ravines, such as the gorges of the Dart and Teign and the dramatic gorge formed by the little River Lyd on the moor's western fringes. These gorges provide some of Dartmoor's most spectacular scenery and most splendid walking country.

The large number of tors that dominate the scene throughout Dartmoor are the remnants of hard masses of granite, drastically reduced in size and moulded into their present shapes by millions of years of weathering. They vary considerably in size and appearance, but the most conspicuous of them – tall ones or those with highly distinctive outlines, such as Bowerman's Nose, Hound Tor, Haytor Rocks, Vixen Tor and many others – are not only impressive but may also act as vital landmarks for walkers in an otherwise featureless landscape. Littering the lower slopes of the hills are smaller granite boulders called, appropriately enough, 'clitters', scooped and gouged from the tors by the action of frost and deposited at random.

Continuous human habitation

As well as this geological 'litter' there is also much historical debris scattered all over Dartmoor, ranging from prehistoric monuments to medieval and later crosses, tin-mine workings, abandoned quarries and the long-disused tracks of 19th-century tramways and railways; evidence both of continuous human occupation and of the long history of industrial exploitation of the moor. This 'man-made' litter may be difficult to disentangle from the 'natural' litter in places where both lie side by side, so easily and quickly does the granite blend into the landscape.

There are few areas in Britain which have a higher concentration of prehistoric monuments than Dartmoor. Although none of these are on the scale of Stonehenge or Maiden Castle, they are extremely atmospheric in their wild and lonely moorland settings. The attractions of Dartmoor to prehistoric settlers – perhaps difficult to understand at first glance – were that its altitude, above the damp and thickly wooded valleys, enabled them to practise simple farming, while there was plenty of granite for building material. In addition, the climate at that time seems to have been warmer and drier. It is the durability of granite coupled with the scarcity of later settlements that has enabled so many of these prehistoric remains to survive. Most of them date from the Bronze Age and include burial chambers, stone circles (such as those at Scorhill and Grey Wethers), avenues of stones (there is a particularly impressive one at Merrivale), standing stones and hut circles. One of the most visited sites is the village at Grimspound, where over twenty hut circles are grouped together, enclosed by a wall.

Later Iron Age peoples were responsible for constructing the hill forts, one of the finest of which is Cranbrook Castle. By the time the Romans arrived in the south west in around AD 50, the native Celtic tribes of Devon and Cornwall

had formed themselves into a confederation called the Dumnonii (from which Devon gets its name), but whether they used those forts against the Roman invaders is uncertain. The Romans certainly established Exeter (*Isca Dumnoniorum*) as their main base in the area, but they seem to have largely left Dartmoor and its inhabitants to their own devices.

During the Dark Ages following the departure of the Romans, Saxon invaders are likely to have penetrated into

Prehistoric remains at Merrivale, overlooked by King's Tor

Dartmoor via the river valleys, establishing small farming communities, but progress, both against the terrain and against fierce Celtic resistance, seems to have been slow, and it was probably not until the 9th century that Devon was incorporated into the Saxon kingdom of Wessex. Alfred the Great made Lydford (on the western edge of the moor, in effect on the western frontier of Wessex, facing both the Celts of Cornwall and marauding Danish invaders) a fortified 'burgh', and the present village still retains its original street pattern and sits within its Saxon earthworks.

Hunting, tin mining and farming

Like the Roman conquerors before them, Norman kings made Exeter an administrative as well as an ecclesiastical centre, but unlike the Romans they viewed Dartmoor as an asset, seeing in its open spaces and rugged terrain an ideal hunting ground. Under William the Conqueror and his successors, therefore, it became a royal forest, and its boundaries were officially marked out in 1204. Links with the Crown were further cemented when in 1239 Henry III granted the Forest of Dartmoor to his brother Richard, Earl of Cornwall, and since then up until the present day a large proportion of the region has been part of the Duchy of Cornwall.

Following the Norman Conquest, castles and monasteries were built around the periphery of Dartmoor – the former at Exeter, Okehampton and Totnes and the latter at Buckfast, Tavistock, Buckland and Plympton. The most important development in Dartmoor's medieval history, however, was the discovery of tin in about the middle of the 12th century, proving one of the richest sources in Europe. Tin mining flourished in the 12th and 13th centuries and had its own laws and customs administered from the four Stannary Towns (from the Latin *stannum,* meaning 'tin') of Tavistock, Plympton, Ashburton and Chagford. 'Stannary Parliaments' were held on Crockern Tor (roughly equidistant from the four towns) and offenders against the laws were tried and imprisoned in Lydford Castle. After another boom in the Tudor era, tin mining declined (the last mine closed in the 20th century), and its relics, scattered around the moor, provide a fertile field for those interested in industrial archaeology.

Monastic activities, the expansion of farming and the development of the tin trade led to a growth in commercial activity and the creation of a number of transmoorland routeways, with crosses and marker-posts to guide travellers across the wilder and more featureless parts of the moor and 'clapper bridges' (simple structures of flat granite slabs) across the rivers and streams as distinctive features. Some of these crosses and posts, both medieval ones and those of a later date, remain, still serving as convenient route guides for walkers on the moor. Examples are Bennett's Cross, between Postbridge and Moretonhampstead on the B3212 (the road itself follows the line of a medieval track), Nun's or Siward's Cross in the Upper Plym valley and the later crosses marked with a 'T' and an 'A' to indicate a route between Tavistock and Ashburton. A few of the clapper bridges survive, notably the one over the East Dart at Postbridge, visible and easily accessible from the main road. Parts of some of these old tracks now make fine long-distance walking routes. One of the best known is the Abbot's Way, which can be followed across southern Dartmoor between the Dart and the Plym. This was believed to be a link between the abbeys of Buckfast in the east and Buckland and Tavistock in the west but there is no definite evidence and the route probably predates the abbeys.

The prison, quarrying, china clay and tourism
Dartmoor remained largely remote and inaccessible, with farming and tin mining the chief activities, until towards the end of the 18th and the

beginning of the 19th centuries, when a number of developments were initiated. The first of these was the foundation of Princetown by Thomas Tyrwhitt, Lord Warden of the Stannaries, who had grand plans to create agricultural land from this, the wettest, bleakest and most barren part of the moor, and to attract people into the area. It was he who suggested the building of the prison in 1806, to house French prisoners from the Napoleonic Wars, who could be employed in preparing the land for farming and quarrying granite. Although at the end of the wars in 1815 the prison closed down (it reopened in 1850 as a convict settlement), while Princetown itself never really developed and Tyrwhitt's agricultural schemes came to nothing, this enterprising if over-ambitious man kept the town going by constructing a tramway (later converted to a railway) to carry granite from the nearby quarries down to Plymouth, for transporting to London and beyond. Parts of this now abandoned line can be traced across the moor around Princetown and Merrivale and make an excellent footpath. In Victorian times, demand for Dartmoor granite as a building material increased and quarrying was greatly expanded. The lines of tramways can still be followed, in particular those that carried granite from the quarries on Haytor Down to Teignmouth, for which the stone setts are still visible.

Other 19th-century developments were the small-scale mining of copper, lead and iron and the creation of a china clay industry, whose workings scar parts of the Plym valley near Shaugh Prior. Around the middle of the century came the first tourists, as Victorian travellers were tempted away from the more genteel pleasures of Torquay and Teignmouth to discover the now fashionable, natural wonders of the moor. Most of these visitors restricted themselves to the southern and eastern parts of the moor, more easily accessible from Exeter and the coast, and both Chagford and Moretonhampstead became tourist centres in their own right.

Water and military training

The wilderness of northern and western Dartmoor attracted attention from other quarters – the water authorities and the Ministry of Defence (MOD). The water authorities of Plymouth and the coastal resorts, which were continuing to expand, saw it as an answer to their water supply problems so a number of reservoirs were constructed in the area; the one at Burrator, built in the 1890s, is generally regarded as one of the most attractive stretches of artificial water in the country. The MOD saw it as an ideal military training ground and from the 1870s onwards occupied a large area south of Okehampton.

During the present century both the water authorities and the MOD have increased their activities and extended their land holding on Dartmoor. More reservoirs have been constructed – the last one at Meldon near Okehampton was completed in 1972 – and after the Second World War the area under military occupation was considerably enlarged. Nowadays the MOD controls over 30,000 acres (12,140 ha), mostly between Okehampton and the

Tavistock–Two Bridges road, used for training exercises and firing practice. The 20th century has also seen the expansion of the china clay industry and the establishment of conifer plantations over large parts of the moor (giving a new meaning to the old title of Dartmoor Forest around Sheepstor, Bellever and Fernworthy) as well as even more visitors to the area and an increasing demand for leisure activities.

The Dartmoor National Park

As one of the few remaining areas of largely unspoilt, uncultivated and untamed country left in the south of England, it was not surprising that in 1951 Dartmoor was designated a national park.

Dartmoor is a region of many varying moods – welcoming and forbidding, gentle and rugged – and walking facilities to match, offering everything from easy rambles by wooded streams to moorland hikes as strenuous and difficult as any in the country. But whatever its mood, Dartmoor makes a superb walking area, with excellent waymarking on the many public rights of way around its fringes as well as open access to much of the central moorland.

Note on Range Danger Areas

None of the walks in this book enters the Range Danger Areas, the boundaries of which are marked by red-and-white poles and noticeboards. There is usually access to most of these areas at weekends and certain other times, but do not on any account enter when red flags are flying from nearby hills; this means that the firing ranges are in use.

It is always advisable to get details of firing times, which are available from National Park Information Centres, some local post offices and police stations.

With the introduction of **'gps enabled' walks,** you will see that this book now includes a list of waypoints alongside the description of the walk. We have included these so that you can enjoy the full benefits of gps should you wish to. Gps is an amazingly useful and entertaining navigational aid, and you do not need to be computer literate to enjoy it.

GPS waypoint co-ordinates add value to your walk. You will now have the extra advantage of introducing 'direction' into your walking which will enhance your leisure walking and make it safer. Use of a gps brings greater confidence and security and you will find you cover ground a lot faster should you need to.

For more detailed information on using your gps, a *Pathfinder Guide* introducing you to gps and digital mapping is now available. *GPS for Walkers*, written by experienced gps teacher and navigation trainer Clive Thomas, is available in bookshops (ISBN 978-0-7117-4445-5) or order online at www.totalwalking.co.uk

Lydford Gorge

		GPS waypoints
Start	Lydford	
Distance	3½ miles (5.6km)	✎ SX 510 847
Approximate time	2 hours	Ⓐ SX 509 845
		Ⓑ SX 501 833
Parking	Lydford	Ⓒ SX 498 836
Refreshments	Pub in Lydford, tearooms at Main and Waterfall Entrances to Lydford Gorge	Ⓓ SX 508 846
Ordnance Survey maps	Landrangers 191 (Okehampton & North Dartmoor) and 201 (Plymouth & Launceston), Explorer 112 (Launceston & Holsworthy)	

Just below the ancient village of Lydford, the River Lyd plunges through a thickly wooded ravine, a wonderland of rocks, cliffs, trees and falls, owned by the National Trust. Although this is only a short and relatively easy walk, there are some steep sections and care must be taken on the narrow rocky paths through the gorge, which can become slippery after wet weather. During the winter months (1 November–31 March) access is restricted and this particular circuit is not possible.

In Anglo-Saxon and early medieval times, Lydford was one of the most important towns in Devon: the most westerly fortified 'burgh' in Alfred the Great's kingdom of Wessex, it was one of four towns which had their own mints, and was an administrative centre for the enforcement both of the Stannary Laws, which governed and settled disputes in the tin-mining industry, and the Forest Laws, which governed the royal forest of Dartmoor. Its comparative remoteness and the rise of nearby Tavistock and Okehampton caused its decline and nowadays it is no more than a small stone village on the western edge of Dartmoor, but it is nonetheless uncommonly attractive, with several interesting features relating to its past. It still sits within its Saxon earth ramparts, and the grim-looking castle remains, a single tower built in 1195 as a prison for

offenders against the Stannary and Forest Laws. Justice seems to have been rough and tin miners were sometimes flung into prison without the formality of a trial.

Next to the castle is the church, a fine solid-looking, 13th to 15th-century building. One of its more unusual features is the grave of George Routledge, a watch-

The spectacular White Lady Waterfall

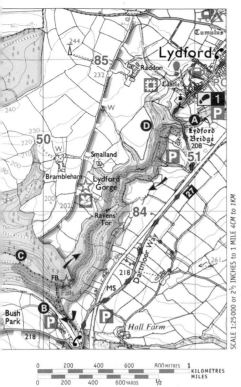

SCALE 1:25000 or 2½ INCHES to 1 MILE 4CM to 1KM

```
0    200   400   600   800 METRES  1
                                      KILOMETRES
                                      MILES
0    200   400   600 YARDS  ½
```

where refreshments are available.

Otherwise turn right at a sign for White Lady Waterfall and, where the paths fork, bear left along the 'Long and Easy' rather than the 'Short and Steep' path. Head gradually downhill, turning sharp right to join the River Lyd at a particularly attractive spot **C**. Keep along the banks of the river, passing an old mine entrance on the right, to the spectacular, 30m (100ft), single-drop White Lady Waterfall. At one time the River Lyd flowed due west from here, along the valley now occupied by the River Burn, but it cut back and broke through into its present steeper valley, flowing northwards and eventually joining the River Tamar, an example of what geographers call river capture.

Opposite the fall cross a footbridge and proceed along the other bank of the Lyd through the increasingly narrow, steep-sided, thickly wooded gorge – an outstandingly beautiful walk, especially on a sunny day with the sun filtering through the foliage. The path here can be quite slippery but there is a handrail available most of the time. Continue on footbridges past the Tunnel Falls, where the turbulent river surges through its narrow and rocky channel by a series of impressive falls. Do not turn right over the first footbridge (signed Short Way Out) but keep ahead through Pixie Glen and follow the path right over the second footbridge **D** to visit the Devil's Cauldron. Here the river makes a deafening noise as its fast-flowing waters swirl around huge boulders that it has carried down, deposited here and literally drilled into the river-bed, a phenomenon called potholing.

Make a short detour to the left for a close-up view of the cauldron but the route follows the right-hand fork uphill, turning right and later left to the exit point and car park. Turn left out of the National Trust car park and retrace your steps over the bridge and along the road back into Lydford village. ●

maker who died in 1802, whose tombstone contains a most amusing epitaph comparing his life with that of a watch.

Start by turning left out of the car park and walk through the village, passing the castle and church on the right, for just over ¼ mile (400m) to Lydford Bridge, from where there is a superb view down into the gorge to the right. Continue over the bridge and turn right **A** into the National Trust car park and shop, where you pay a fee to visit the gorge.

Follow the path downhill, with the tearoom on the right, to pass a 'Way In' board. Follow a winding stepped path down through woodland, turning left at a pink-tipped signpost saying 'Waterfall Entrance'. The path continues above the edge of the gorge for nearly 1 mile (1.6km) before turning right over a footbridge and continuing up steps and through a gate **B** to a signpost. A short detour left here, under a disused railway bridge, leads to the Waterfall Entrance,

Haytor

Start	Haytor
Distance	3½ miles (5.6km)
Approximate time	2 hours
Parking	Hilltop car park off the Bovey Tracey–Widecombe in the Moor road near Haytor
Refreshments	None
Ordnance Survey maps	Landranger 191 (Okehampton & North Dartmoor), Explorer OL28 (Dartmoor)

GPS waypoints

- 🖊 SX 759 767
- Ⓐ SX 758 771
- Ⓑ SX 761 777
- Ⓒ SX 757 777
- Ⓓ SX 755 782
- Ⓔ SX 753 776
- Ⓕ SX 751 775
- Ⓖ SX 751 768

Haytor is the most visited, best known and best loved landmark on Dartmoor, its steep and distinctive twin rocks rising 457m (1490ft) above Haytor Down almost like a British equivalent of Australia's Ayers Rock. As well as providing extensive views and fresh and invigorating walking, Haytor Down possesses a number of interesting relics of Dartmoor's industrial past, as this short but fascinating walk quickly reveals.

🖊 Start by walking straight ahead up to the two rock towers that make up the tor and immediately there are magnificent views: southwards across rolling country to the coast and the Teign estuary and northwards, across a tor and boulder-strewn landscape, into the heart of Dartmoor. The main reasons why Haytor is the most popular landmark in Dartmoor, apart from its distinctive shape, are not only that it is accessible but that it is also possible to climb to the top of the outcrops, from where the views are even more extensive and magnificent. If you attempt this, however, take great care in wet and slippery conditions.

Bear right to pass below the right-hand stack, keeping it on the left. Bear right Ⓐ and head downhill towards the disused Haytor Quarries, soon seen on the left, bordered by a wire fence. Quarries are not usually attractive, but this one is an exception on account of the trees that

have grown up and the pools that have formed within it, which together with some abandoned machinery, give it a strange kind of melancholic beauty. (Keep the fence on the left and you will reach a gate giving access to the quarries if you desire a closer look.) Continue past spoil heaps at the lower end of the quarry and turn left along the granite tramway, easily distinguishable by the stone setts in the turf. This was a horse-drawn tramway, the earliest in Dartmoor, opened in 1820 to transport granite from the local quarries down to the Stover Canal and thence downstream to the port of Teignmouth. It was abandoned in 1858.

Follow this tramway as it bears right and heads in a north-easterly direction to a junction Ⓑ. Here turn sharp left to follow another section of it across the down. At the end of a straight section through a shallow cutting the tramway bears slightly left; turn right Ⓒ and follow the path straight ahead towards the prominent group of rocks called Smallacombe Rocks. The going is flat and relatively easy through heather and bracken. On reaching the rocks bear left, keeping the rocks on your right, and walk to the north end from where there are outstanding views: across the valley of Becka Brook to Greator Rocks and the dramatic pile of Hound Tor beyond with Haytor, as always, dominating the land-scape behind. There are some remains of prehistoric hut circles to the right.

From the north end turn left **D** on a narrow path and make for Holwell Quarries, clearly visible to the right of Haytor, first heading along a path in the direction of the tor and later bearing right through bracken towards the left end of the quarry, to meet the granite tramway **E**. (To take a closer look at the quarry turn right and follow the tramway to its terminus; then retrace your steps to **E** and turn right uphill.) Cross the tramway

The remains of the granite tramway across Haytor Down

and follow the path opposite steeply uphill to gain the scattered outcrops of Holwell Tor **F**, from where there are superb views in all directions.

At the top bear left in a southerly direction towards Emsworthy Rocks, the next prominent outcrop that can be seen ahead on the skyline. As you proceed, Haytor is on the left and the Bovey Tracey-Widecombe road can be seen straight ahead beyond the rocks. Drop into a shallow depression, almost in line with Haytor, then bear right on the path to climb gently towards the rocks on the slight ridge in front. On reaching the top there is a fine view ahead of Saddle Tor.

Turn left **G** along the ridge between stacks of rock, later following a broad green path downhill, then bearing right below the flanks of Haytor Down to the road and car park. From this path there are more glorious views ahead towards the coast. ●

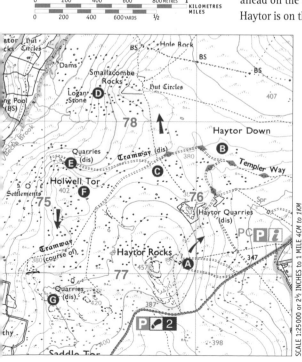

SCALE 1:25000 or 2½ INCHES to 1 MILE 4CM to 1KM

Castle Drogo and Teign Gorge

Start	Fingle Bridge	**GPS waypoints**	
Distance	4 miles (6.4km)	🥾 SX 743 899	
Approximate time	2 hours	Ⓐ SX 728 899	
		Ⓑ SX 726 902	
Parking	Car park just over Fingle Bridge	Ⓒ SX 720 901	
Refreshments	Pub at Fingle Bridge, café and restaurant at Castle Drogo	Ⓓ SX 721 895	
Ordnance Survey maps	Landranger 191 (Okehampton & North Dartmoor), Explorer OL28 (Dartmoor)		

From the picturesque, 16th-century Fingle Bridge over the Teign, the route climbs along the rim of the Teign Gorge, passing the spectacular Castle Drogo, before plunging into the thickly wooded and steep-sided gorge, returning to the bridge via the riverbank. For the first part of this short but exceptionally attractive walk you follow the Hunter's Path; the last part is along the Fisherman's Path.

🥾 From the car park walk back over Fingle Bridge along the lane to Drewsteignton. At a bridleway sign to Hunter's Path turn sharp left, climb steadily through the trees and, after a while, the path emerges into more open country and levels off, giving striking views over the Teign Gorge and the moors beyond. At a footpath sign, keep left along the main path that runs along the top of the gorge across heather, gorse and fern (this is the Hunter's Path).

Soon Castle Drogo comes into view, high up ahead. Ignore the first turning right signed to Castle Drogo/Piddledown Common. Keep ahead along the path; if you want to make a short detour to the castle take the next right turn Ⓐ near the exceptionally fine viewpoint of Sharp Tor. Head up steps and follow the path up to find the main drive where you turn left then right for the NT car park, café, shop and entrance.

Despite its name and its formidable appearance when seen from a distance, Castle Drogo is definitely not a castle; it was in fact built mainly between 1910 and 1930, one of the last country houses to be built on a grand scale before such places became unfashionable and impossibly expensive both to build and maintain. The massive, austere-looking granite house was designed by Sir Edwin Lutyens for his friend, Julius Drewe, a self-made grocery magnate, who chose this spot both for its commanding position above the Teign Gorge and because he thought there might be a connection between his name and nearby Drewsteignton. In 1974 it was given to the National Trust. The interior is a maze of fascinating rooms and passages and from the gardens there are fine views of the castle itself, the gorge below and hills and moorlands beyond.

Retrace your steps along the drive and

The delightful, thickly wooded gorge of the River Teign below Castle Drogo

turn right down the path **B**. Keep ahead downhill at a fork, then bear right down steps to rejoin the Hunter's Path. Turn right; eventually the path descends gradually, turning sharply right at Hunter's Tor, the westerly edge of the Teign Gorge, continuing steeply downhill through woodland to a gate and footpath sign to the Fisherman's Path **C**. Turn left along a downhill track, bearing left away from that track at a public footpath sign and bearing left again to the river **D**.

Turn left along the Fisherman's Path, which keeps by the Teign through the thickly wooded gorge back to Fingle Bridge, a distance of under 2 miles (3.2km). The route is fairly easy except at one point where the path has to climb up and down some steps across the lower reaches of Sharp Tor. ●

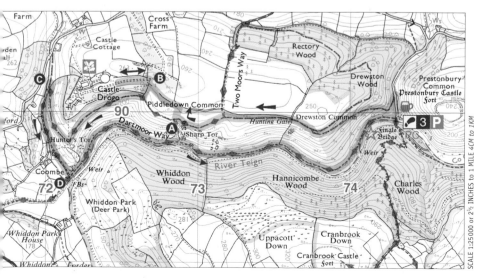

Plym Woods and Wigford Down

		GPS waypoints	
Start	Shaugh Bridge		
Distance	4 miles (6.4km)	📷	SX 533 636
Approximate time	2 hours	**A**	SX 555 646
		B	SX 555 647
Parking	Car park beside Shaugh Bridge	**C**	SX 537 639
Refreshments	None	**D**	SX 537 642
Ordnance Survey maps	Landrangers 201 (Plymouth & Launceston) and 202 (Torbay & South Dartmoor), Explorer OL28 (Dartmoor)		

Relics of two of Dartmoor's former major industries, quarrying and china clay, feature prominently in this relatively easy walk, along with some beautiful stretches of woodland, fresh and open downland and fine views over both moorland and coast, including nearby Plymouth. The route traverses a particularly attractive section of the Plym valley between Shaugh Bridge and Cadover Bridge – the first half is above or through Plym Woods on the south side of the river and the second half takes you across Wigford Down on the north side, passing the superb viewpoint of the Dewerstone Rock.

Shaugh Bridge lies just below the confluence of the Plym and the Meavy and, after heavy rain, their combined waters make a most impressive sight as they surge below the bridge and over rocks between the steep, wooded hillsides.

📷 The walk begins near the car park entrance, where there are some steps by the side of the remains of drying-kilns from the china clay industry. Climb these, walk along the path towards the road and, at a public footpath sign to Cadover Bridge, turn left through woodland, walk uphill to climb a stile and keep ahead, climbing quite steeply through a tangle of trees and rocks. A brief level section through open country reveals fine views to the right across Bickleigh Down towards Plymouth and the coast. The path

then bears left and starts to climb again, re-entering woodland; where a wire fence appears ahead bear left.

For the next $1\frac{1}{2}$ miles (2.4km) you keep along the Pipe Track, a footpath partly above and partly through the Plym valley woodlands. This follows the line of an old underground pipe that carried china clay from where it was mined near Cadover Bridge to the drying-kilns at Shaugh Bridge and, for much of the way, sections of the broken pipe can be seen, serving as a useful landmark. Initially there is an excellent view of the perpendicular faces of the Dewerstone Rock on the opposite side of the river and, further on, across Wigford Down to the high moors beyond. After proceeding above the top edge of the woods, climb a stile to enter North

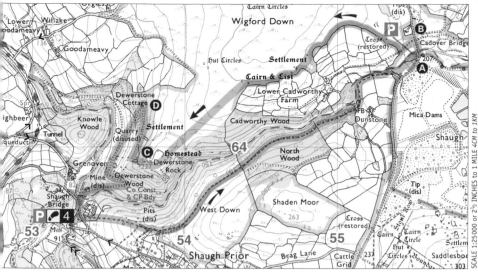

```
0      200    400    600    800 METRES  1
                                        KILOMETRES
                                        MILES
0      200    400    600 YARDS   1/2
```

Wood and continue along the Pipe Track, gradually drawing closer to the turbulent waters of the Plym. Climb a succession of stiles, eventually emerging from the woods through a gate; keep ahead across the car park to join the road near Cadover Bridge, situated at the point where the Plym tumbles off the open moor to proceed through more wooded country towards Plymouth Sound.

Turn left over the bridge **A** and look upstream: to the right are the white spoil-tips of china clay workings and ahead is a fine view of wild and bare moorland, making a striking contrast to the thickly wooded terrain just traversed. After crossing the bridge, turn left onto a track **B**, then bear right on a grassy path that heads up to a cross, discovered, restored and re-erected here in 1873 by troops exercising in the locality. Keep ahead uphill onto Wigford Down, keeping close to the field boundary walls on the left, along a good, clear path that cuts a swathe through the bracken which covers much of the down, giving excellent views all the way.

After a while the path curves to the left, still following the line of boundary walls, in a south-westerly direction. Eventually the wall bears away left and the sheer cliffs of Dewerstone Rock come into view ahead. Keep ahead, passing a prominent group of rocks on the left, and continue along the ridge to the notable viewpoint on the tor **C** above the Dewerstone. The view from here across the wooded valley to Plymouth and the coast in the distance is outstanding.

Continue over the rock and drop downhill on a narrow grassy path, crossing a wall to enter Dewerstone Wood, bearing right and heading in a northerly direction, later bearing right again through a disused quarry. All around, half-hidden amongst the trees, are relics of the quarrying industry. Eventually you reach the granite sleepers and the ruined cable brake drumhouse of an early 19th-century inclined tramway. Turn sharp left **D** down the tramway and head down to a lower section. Keep straight on, eventually passing more quarries. Where the path forks keep right, downhill, on the granite-paved path, ignoring a path left towards the base of the Dewerstone. Soon the River Plym is seen below left, and the path leads to a wooden footbridge just above the confluence with the River Meavy. Cross the footbridge over the Plym to return to the car park. ●

Lustleigh Cleave

		GPS waypoints	
Start	Lustleigh	🥾	SX 784 812
Distance	5 miles (8km)	**Ⓐ**	SX 785 813
Approximate time	2½ hours	**Ⓑ**	SX 781 813
Parking	Roadside parking in Lustleigh	**Ⓒ**	SX 774 816
Refreshments	Pubs and tearooms in Lustleigh	**Ⓓ**	SX 760 824
Ordnance Survey maps	Landranger 191 (Okehampton &	**Ⓔ**	SX 758 828
	North Dartmoor),	**Ⓕ**	SX 757 820
	Explorer OL28 (Dartmoor)	**Ⓖ**	SX 772 812
		Ⓗ	SX 779 809

'Cleave' is a local word for valley and Lustleigh Cleave refers to a particularly attractive part of the Bovey valley lying to the west of Lustleigh village. The first half of the walk is along the top edge of the Cleave, giving extensive views and passing impressive granite outcrops; the second half is through the dense woodland, and, at times, thick bracken which clothe the lower slopes and valley bottom.

In many ways Lustleigh is everyone's idea of what the perfect English village should look like, and the old cottages and thatched inn grouped around the village green and church make a delightful composition. The perpendicular church dates mainly from the 13th to 16th centuries and among its many interesting features is a fine screen dating from Mary I's reign.

🥾 Keeping the church on the right, walk towards the post office and village stores. Turn right and follow the lane uphill around the church wall. Turn left at the junction, and left again at the war memorial along an uphill lane **Ⓐ**. In a few yards, where the lane bears right, bear left at a public footpath sign along a private drive. At the end pass to the right of a house along a narrow path to reach a kissing-gate. Go through and bear left, with a hedge to the left, down to a hunting gate. Pass through and keep ahead, through a wood, over a stream and up to a lane **Ⓑ**. Turn right and follow the

lane very steeply uphill, through a farm, eventually to reach a T-junction.

Turn right (fine views here over to the right) and, at a public bridleway sign for Cleave, Foxworthy and Hunter's Tor, turn left **Ⓒ** along a sunken path between hedge-banks to a gate and another public bridleway sign. Here keep straight ahead, following the sign for Hunter's Tor, along a path which climbs through woods, past huge rocks almost hidden by trees and undergrowth (a feature of the landscape in this part of Dartmoor), eventually emerging at the summit of Sharpitor. There was once a large stone balanced on the edge of the tor here, called the Nut Crackers, unfortunately prised over the edge by drunken vandals in 1951 and damaged in the fall. Efforts to put it back only resulted in further damage and the attempt was abandoned.

Now take the path (right) along the top edge of Lustleigh Cleave, with superb views over the thickly wooded valley on the left and the tower of Manaton church and Hound Tor. The path continues for 1 mile (1.6km) through bracken and heather, with magnificent views southwards towards the coast, Haytor and Hound Tor to the west, and the gently rolling country on the fringes of Dartmoor to the east. Eventually the path reaches a gate in a wall ahead. To the left is Hunter's Tor; to the right the outlines of an Iron Age fort; to the north fabulous views over the villages of North Bovey and Moretonhampstead, with the bleaker high moorlands beyond.

Go through the gate and bear right **D**. Follow the narrow path downhill, parallel to a wall on the right, to reach a footpath sign. Here turn sharp left downhill. Go through the next gate and immediately right through another. Continue down the right edge of the next field to reach a gate, with a farm right. Go through the gate and straight on down the concrete lane. Where this bears right – at a three-way fingerpost **E** – turn left through a gate, following directions for Foxworthy Bridge. This lovely track winds along the lower slopes of the Bovey valley, negotiating two gates before reaching the hamlet at Foxworthy. Turn right downhill towards Foxworthy Bridge over the River Bovey.

Do not cross the bridge but turn left **F** just before it, at a public bridleway sign to Hammerslake, along a broad track following public bridleway signs all the time. It is fortunate that this part of the route is so well waymarked because the next 1$\frac{1}{2}$ miles (2.4km) is mainly along

Cottages cluster around the church at Lustleigh

narrow paths, either through dense woodland or across tall bracken, normally difficult terrain for route finding. Go through a gate, after which the path becomes narrower as it winds through pretty oak woodland. At a signpost 'Hammerslake for Lustleigh' keep ahead along the side of the thickly wooded cleave. This lovely path undulates through woodland and bracken, accompanied by sounds of the rushing waters of the River Bovey below right, and with intermittent views over the valley to Hound Tor. Eventually the path climbs uphill to reach a T-junction of paths with a wall ahead **G**. Turn right here and head steeply downhill to another path sign and keep

ahead. Keep ahead again (left) where a small path joins from the right. The path continues through oak woodland. At the next footpath sign bear left uphill, signed Lustleigh, and soon after reach a gate. Go through and continue between hedgebanks to reach a track; follow this downhill to reach a lane **H**.

Turn right and take the first turning on the left into Pethybridge. Walk through the hamlet, passing some delightful thatched cottages and, just before a postbox, turn right along a lane which heads downhill, later bending sharply right and then left. Soon a fine view opens up of the houses and church of Lustleigh. At a T-junction, turn right along another narrow lane, turning left at the next T-junction and heading straight back to the village centre. ●

0	200	400	600	800 METRES	1
					KILOMETRES
0	200	400	600 YARDS	½	MILES

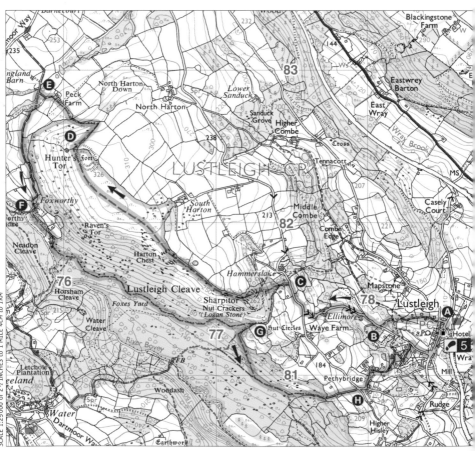

SCALE 1:25 000 or 2½ INCHES to 1 MILE 4CM to 1KM

Steps Bridge and Mardon Down

			GPS waypoints
Start	Steps Bridge		🥾 SX 803 883
Distance	7½ miles (12.1km)		Ⓐ SX 800 873
Approximate time	3½ hours		Ⓑ SX 789 870
Parking	Car park at Steps Bridge		Ⓒ SX 788 875
Refreshments	Pub and café in Dunsford (off route)		Ⓓ SX 783 880
Ordnance Survey maps	Landranger 191 (Okehampton & North Dartmoor), Explorer OL28 (Dartmoor)		Ⓔ SX 771 878
			Ⓕ SX 780 898

This is a fine walk at any time of the year, but particularly in the spring, when woodland and meadows along the Teign are ablaze with daffodils. Wild flowers are also a feature of the opening section of the walk, which climbs through Bridford Wood. Mardon Down offers a taste of open downland with fine views eastwards towards the high moors.

🥾 From the car park at Steps Bridge, turn left and walk a few yards down the road. Turn right into Bridford Wood and keep ahead up a track to a signpost. Walk straight ahead on a public bridleway up through the wood, soon crossing a bridge over a stream. The abundance of wild flowers here in season reminds us that this is a conservation area.

The path continues uphill, parallel to a stream, eventually bearing left to cross it by stepping stones. Immediately turn right – the path steepens – at a public bridleway signpost to Burnicombe. The dedicated conservation area ends at the National Trust sign.

Continue up the left bank of the stream and through a gate at the top. Follow the bridlepath (marked blue), across the stream (on the right) again. Continue uphill and through a wooden gate

Daffodil time in Dunsford Wood

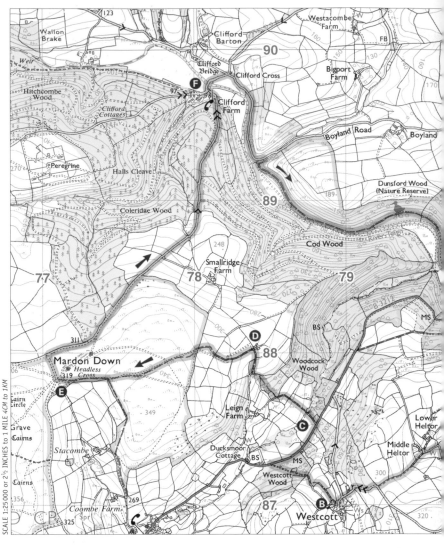

0	200	400	600	800 METRES	1	
						KILOMETRES
						MILES
0	200	400	600 YARDS	½		

at the top of the field onto an ancient track. This leads to the edge of Burnicombe farmyard, where there is a choice of routes **A**.

Keep straight on if you wish to climb Heltor Rock. In this case you will have to use ¾ mile (1.2km) of roadway.

Otherwise turn right onto the footpath to Thorn, which is waymarked yellow. Pass through a metal gate, keeping the hedge on the right through the first field,

then through another metal gate. Keep the hedge on the left; about 50 yds (46m) along the hedgerow you will find a well-concealed stile. Cross this, noting an ancient gatepost.

Continue right (with a fence on the right) and cross another stile. Keep along the lower edge of the next field, with views of Heltor left. Pass through a gate and bear left to go through another to reach the farmyard at Thorn. Keep ahead to reach a lane via another gate. Turn right to Middle Heltor and, just before a house on the left, turn left up a narrow

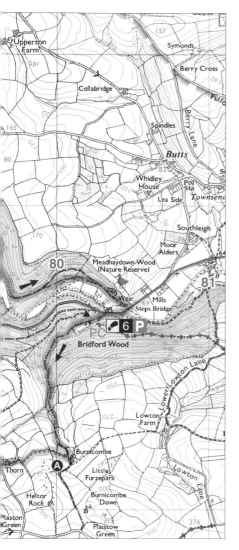

into a meadow and keep well to the left to find a stile facing a wood. This gives access to an ancient track between mossy stone walls. Turn right and follow this downhill and through a gate to enter Westcott Wood. Bear left and follow the path down to reach the road.

Turn right; after about ½ mile (800m), but before the wood begins, look for a bridleway sign by a metal gate on the left **C** with a house opposite. Go through and continue downhill to cross a stream at the bottom.

The arduous climb to Mardon Down now begins. Keep to the left of the meadow, and straight on through a wooden gate onto a track. Turn right through a wooden gate to leave the track before reaching Leign Farm. Climb to the top of the woods and through a gate in the wall. Follow the path to another gate onto a farm track. Turn right, then left by farm buildings **D** along an unsignposted and sunken green lane, through a metal gate.

Keep on climbing, pausing to look back left to Heltor, before reaching the plateau of Mardon Down through a gate.

Follow the broad, grassy track straight ahead to reach Headless Cross **E** in the midst of the heath. Turn right onto the lane, bearing right at the next junction; follow the lane as it descends steeply to reach Clifford Bridge – a long stretch.

Turn right to cross the bridge **F**, and right again at the next junction. Where the lane bears left away from the river, take the bridlepath on the right to Steps Bridge, where in the springtime there are spectacular views of the Teign through fields of wild daffodils. Later in the year, the foliage makes an equally colourful picture. At times a footpath breaks away right from the bridlepath to run nearer the river; notices ask visitors to be aware of erosion problems along the riverbank. The Devon Wildlife Trust manages these woodlands for the National Trust. Turn right over Steps Bridge to return to the car park. ●

green lane with an orchard on the right. This climbs to reach a wooden gate. Keeping the fence on your right, continue to climb up the field.

At the top look for a stile (marked with yellow and partly screened by gorse bushes) in the right-hand corner. Cross this, then another, to reach a lane. Turn right and descend to Westcott **B**.

At the T-junction turn left, towards a 'dead end' sign. After 20 yds (18m) turn right on a footpath to the B3212. Climb the short, steep track, then follow a sign right into a short green lane. Cross a stile

Burrator reservoir and Sheeps Tor

Start	Burrator reservoir	GPS waypoints	
Distance	5½ miles (8.9km)		SX 569 693
Approximate time	3 hours	Ⓐ	SX 565 689
		Ⓑ	SX 565 682
Parking	Car park by Norsworthy Bridge at eastern end of reservoir	Ⓒ	SX 560 680
		Ⓓ	SX 558 675
Refreshments	Pub at Meavy	Ⓔ	SX 551 669
Ordnance Survey maps	Landrangers 201 (Plymouth & Launceston) and 202 (Torbay & South Dartmoor), Explorer OL28 (Dartmoor)	Ⓕ	SX 544 671
		Ⓖ	SX 550 680

The level final leg of this walk along the road that skirts the northern shore of the reservoir will be welcomed by those who have found the earlier stages (and especially the ascent of Sheeps Tor) somewhat energetic. The views from the top, however, are well worth the climb, and the ensuing amble through quiet lanes, fields and woodland is quite delightful.

Leave the car park and turn left onto the road to skirt the eastern end of the reservoir, which is some way distant. The road bends westwards, passing the parking area for Burrator arboretum on the left. As the southern shore of the lake is reached, turn left up a waymarked forest track Ⓐ. Pass through a gap in a wall to reach a signpost on the edge of moorland; bear slightly right (unsigned) and climb steeply uphill, initially with a wall to the left, to gain the top of Sheeps Tor. This is well worth the strenuous climb, being one of Dartmoor's finest viewpoints. The reservoir immediately below gives scale to the panorama and relieves the desolation of the moor. Make your way to the southern summit of Sheeps Tor Ⓑ. Descend steeply on a clear grassy path, passing a stone water board pillar en route, heading for a strip of conifers at the south-east corner of the reservoir. Pass through the

gate Ⓒ at the bottom to an intake, leading to a lane. Turn left, then left again, to Sheepstor village, with its lovely church, rebuilt in the early 16th century.

By the cross in front of the church turn right down a narrow lane. Cross a stream; 50 yds (46m) later take a footpath on the right Ⓓ signposted to Marchant's Cross through a gate. At the end of the track cross the field diagonally left to a metal gate, and then another. Now keep the

---

Burrator reservoir, with Leather Tor beyond

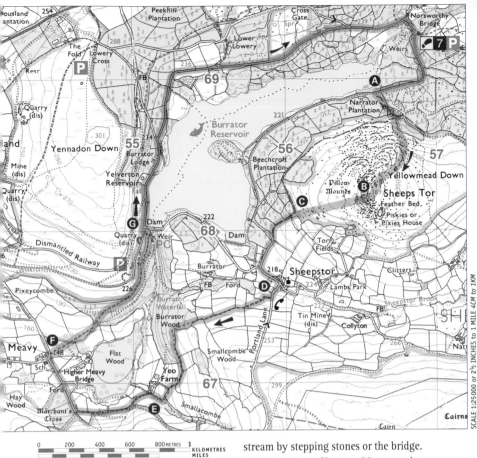

SCALE 1:25000 or 2½ INCHES to 1 MILE 4CM to 1KM

0	200	400	600	800 METRES	1
					KILOMETRES
					MILES
0	200	400	600 YARDS	½	

hedge on the right, following yellow waymarking on stones and electricity poles. Cross a wall via stone steps, and two stiles to enter oak woods; the path is marked with yellow splodges. At the end of the wood, climb the wall on the left and descend an enclosed path. A lovely view opens up right towards Meavy. Follow the footpath sign right down a track, pass through a gate and then bear left over a stile. The fenced-in path skirts a field and drops downhill. A stile leads to a descent through woodland, by a dried-up stream bed. A stile, footbridge and further stile lead onto a lane opposite beautiful Yeo Farm **E**, with the date when it was built, 1610, on the porch.

Turn left along the lane to reach Marchant's Cross. Turn right and cross the stream by stepping stones or the bridge. Pass a junction of lanes at Meavy, and turn right through a gate at a footpath sign **F**. Keep straight across a meadow, with picturesque clusters of oak trees, and pass through two gates; then bear left on a twisting path through the trees, following yellow marks. This leads to the dried-up leat that was built in the 16th century to provide Plymouth with a water supply. At this point you will hear the sound of Burrator Waterfall, coming from the depths of the gorge below. The path follows the leat for some way before meeting a track on a U-bend; follow the track left, uphill, to emerge on the Dousland road just below the dam. Turn right to pass the dam **G** and follow the road up the west then north side of the reservoir back to the car park. Small stiles over the fence on the right-hand side allow closer vistas of Burrator. ●

Chagford and the River Teign

Start	Chagford		GPS waypoints
Distance	4 miles (6.4m)		SX 702 874
Approximate time	2 hours		Ⓐ SX 701 870
Parking	Car park above Chagford church		Ⓑ SX 709 865
Refreshments	Pubs and cafés in Chagford		Ⓒ SX 711 872
Ordnance Survey maps	Landranger 191 (Okehampton & North Dartmoor), Explorer OL28 (Dartmoor)		Ⓓ SX 710 878
			Ⓔ SX 706 881
			Ⓕ SX 705 882
			Ⓖ SX 693 879

A pleasant walk with a steep, tough start uphill onto Nattadon Common. The rest of the walk passes through woodland and along the banks of the lovely River Teign.

Chagford, a former stannary town, is a most attractive place, full of interesting shops and pubs and with a church that is well worth visiting.

🖊 Turn left out of the car park, and then turn left again along New Street so that you are heading southwards out of the village. Cottages line the narrow street, most of them with carefully tended window boxes and hanging baskets.

Just before the lane descends bear left Ⓐ up a tarmac way. Between houses at the crest turn left following a footpath sign to Nattadon Common. This climb is steep. Make the ascent, with a wall and wood on the left, to reach the col. Meet a road and bear right, and continue straight ahead (ignoring the turn to the right) to find a

Chagford's delightful market house

bridlepath junction where the road bends to the left. Turn sharp left **B** onto the footpath here (Great Weeke and Yellam). The path drops down quite steeply. Keep the hedgebank on your left to reach a narrow path at the bottom – a perfect and obviously ancient path. This old way is soon abandoned, however, and the route passes through a gate and along a field path, which descends gently to pass through a gate into a wood.

In the wood turn left at the footpath junction **C**, climbing a stile, towards Westcott. In spring the path threads through bluebells. Cross the stile and the stream at the bottom to enter a wood and then up steps to cross another stile and stream. Bear right to reach a farm track and follow this to reach a road via another stile.

Turn right and follow the winding lane past thatched Westcott Farm on the left. Bear left at a junction and pass Adley

House. Within 100 yds (92m) there is a footpath on the left **D** which crosses two fields diagonally via stiles to emerge amidst modern houses. Keep ahead along a track to meet a road. Turn left **E** along the road; 100 yds (92m) later turn right over a stile onto a footpath. Cross a field, bearing left to pass through a small gate to meet a lane; turn right **F** to cross Rushford Bridge. Take the footpath on the left to Chagford Bridge. A footbridge across an old mill leat leads to a footpath by the side of the river. This path also passes through bluebells. As Chagford Bridge is approached, notice how the trunks of the oak trees are protected by stone walls. On meeting the road turn left **G** to cross the bridge, later bearing left again and continuing uphill to return to the village. ●

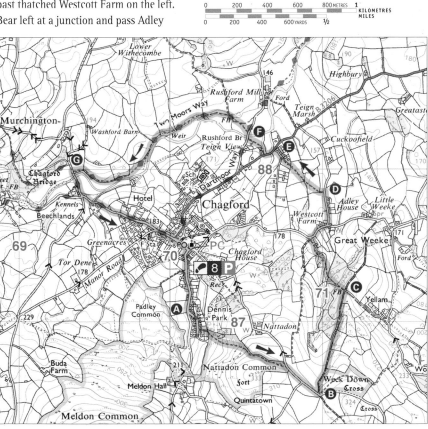

SCALE 1:25000 or 2½ INCHES to 1 MILE 4CM to 1KM

South Brent and the Avon valley

Start	South Brent		GPS waypoints
Distance	5½ miles (8.9km)		🖉 SX 698 602
Approximate time	3 hours		Ⓐ SX 695 606
Parking	South Brent		Ⓑ SX 691 607
Refreshments	Pubs in South Brent		Ⓒ SX 683 608
Ordnance Survey maps	Landranger 202 (Torbay & South Dartmoor), Explorer OL28 (Dartmoor)		Ⓓ SX 670 612
			Ⓔ SX 679 623
			Ⓕ SX 681 627
			Ⓖ SX 685 622
			Ⓗ SX 696 612

This walk explores a section of the Avon valley, on the southern fringe of the moor between South Brent and Shipley Bridge, and provides a striking contrast between the gentle, wooded country by the river itself and the wilder and more open terrain to the east, west and north. It is an easy walk to follow, but bear in mind that much of the route between Ⓑ and Ⓓ is steadily uphill.

South Brent is one of those places that can be described either as a large village or as a small market town. Its church is unusual in that it was originally a small cruciform building, with the Norman tower (the oldest part) at the centre instead of, as now, at the west end. The western arm of the church was demolished in the 12th century and the church was extended eastwards at intervals during the 13th, 14th and 15th centuries to assume its present size and shape.

🖉 Turn right out of the car park up to the church, cross the road and, at a public footpath sign to Lydia Bridge, turn right along a path that heads down under the railway bridge. Go through a kissing-gate and follow the delightful, tree-shaded banks of the River Avon for ¼ mile (400m) to Lydia Bridge Ⓐ, where the river surges through rocks above and below the half-hidden bridge, making an attractive scene. Turn left over the bridge and keep along a

lane for just over ¼ mile (400m) through the hamlet of Aish and, just where the lane bends sharply to the right, turn left by a letterbox Ⓑ and continue between houses along a broad, hedge-lined track.

Follow this winding track for ¾ mile (1.2km) up to a gate, onto open grassland. Go through and turn left at a public bridleway sign Ⓒ along a path (keeping left at the fork) across Aish Ridge, heading west. The path descends through bracken and gorse, bearing right to join an enclosed track. From the ridge there are fine and extensive views, especially to the right over Brent Moor towards the head of the Avon valley. Go through a gate, keep ahead to two gates and, passing through the left-hand one, continue along an uphill enclosed track to Ball Gate Ⓓ.

Here go through three gates in quick succession, bearing right after the third one to follow a public bridleway sign to Shipley Bridge via Diamond Lane. With

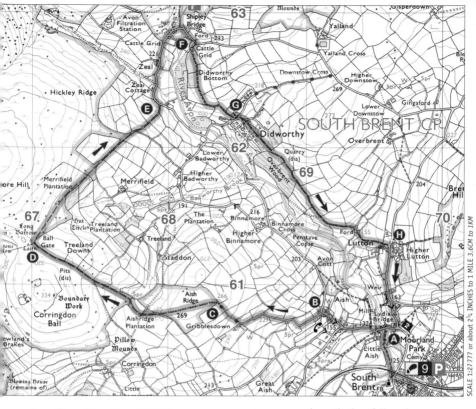

SCALE 1:27 777 or about 2¼ INCHES to 1 MILE 3.6CM to 1KM

0   200   400   600   800 METRES **1**
  KILOMETRES
  MILES
0   200   400   600 YARDS   ½

sweeping views all around, strike out in a
north-easterly direction across open
moorland, heading away from the wall on
the right, towards Merrifield Plantation
ahead. Here pick up another wall on the
right, keep by it and, where it ends,
continue ahead to join a wide, green,
walled path that heads down into the
Avon valley, following a wall on the right.
Go through a gate and down a narrow,
enclosed, rocky path to another gate and
onto a lane **E**. Turn left and follow the
lane to pass the car park at Shipley Bridge.

Keep along the lane to cross the bridge
and shortly afterwards, just after a cattle-
grid, turn right at a public footpath sign to
Lutton via Didworthy **F**. Go through a
gate and keep ahead to a stile. Climb over
and bear slightly left uphill; the path
levels and runs through woodland to
eventually cross a stile. Follow the path

on to cross another stile then follow the
rocky path downhill to a gate **G**. Go
through and cross the lane; continue
ahead on a tarmac track to the hamlet of
Didworthy.

Bear right, passing a house on the left,
along an uphill tarmac lane (later a rough
track), which keeps above the Avon valley.
At the gates of a house, bear slightly left
along a much narrower path between
hedges, along the top edge of Overbrent
Wood on the right, to a gate. Go through
and, with a wall to the right, keep ahead,
pass through another gate and continue
along a green path, lined with trees and
hedges, dropping down to go through yet
another gate. Keep ahead to descend to a
ford, then follow the track uphill into the
hamlet of Lutton. On meeting a lane keep
ahead uphill to a T-junction **H**.

Turn right along the lane and follow it
for ½ mile (800m) to a T-junction. Turn
right to find Lydia Bridge. Here retrace your
steps by the Avon back to South Brent. ●

The Walkham valley and Merrivale

Start	Merrivale	**GPS waypoints**	
Distance	5½ miles (8.9km)	🥾 SX 553 750	
Approximate time	2½ hours	Ⓐ SX 550 750	
		Ⓑ SX 546 722	
Parking	Unmarked parking area on left side of the Two Bridges–Tavistock road, just above Merrivale Bridge	Ⓒ SX 555 725	
		Ⓓ SX 560 729	
		Ⓔ SX 557 740	
Refreshments	Dartmoor Inn at Merrivale	Ⓕ SX 556 747	
Ordnance Survey maps	Landranger 191 (Okehampton & North Dartmoor), Explorer OL28 (Dartmoor)		

As well as fine and varied views, both across the wooded Walkham valley and over wild and open moorland, this is a walk with much of historic interest, ranging from a group of Bronze Age remains to early 19th-century industrial archaeology. Although this relatively easy route involves little climbing, there are parts that may be muddy and others where the terrain is rough with no visible paths; it is therefore advisable not to attempt this walk in poor visibility.

🥾 Walk down the road towards the river and turn left, just before the bridge Ⓐ, on a public bridlepath. Go through a gate and keep ahead along a good wide track, passing a disused quarry on the left. To the right, on the other side of the river, Vixen Tor, the tallest and one of the most impressive of Dartmoor's many granite outcrops, stands out. Keep ahead through a farm, and another gate (farmhouse left). Pass through a further gate and along the right edge of moorland. Cross the stream to enter woodland. Continue through the woods, passing Hucken Tor, where a gate has been built between the rocks of the tor. The views over the Walkham valley on the right, towards the church at Sampford Spiney, are outstanding. The path keeps fairly straight, through several gates, later joining a narrow tarmac lane at Daveytown.

At a crossroads Ⓑ turn left (signposted Criptor) uphill, go through a gate by a cattle-grid and keep straight ahead along a track below Ingra Tor on the right. Pass through another gate and head across open moorland. As the track bears left towards a farm, cross a stream; immediately turn left Ⓒ across rough grassland on a signed bridleway, conveniently marked by occasional posts with blue splashes. Cross a stream (at times of high water go slightly upstream to a narrower crossing point) and, still following blue waymarks, head uphill. As the land rises through a tangle of rocks and gorse, and a wire fence comes into view above, take the left of two grassy paths and continue uphill to a gate in a fence.

Go through and turn left Ⓓ along the track of a disused railway, passing the abandoned Swelltor quarries on the right.

The railway was originally built by Sir Thomas Tyrwhitt, founder of nearby Princetown, as a horse-drawn tramway in the 1820s, and was later converted to a steam-driven railway. It mainly carried granite from the many quarries in the locality and was closed down in 1956. Keep along this disused track for 1 mile (1.6km) following it as it curves to the right through a cutting, where you can see that the line of the original horse-drawn tramway diverges from that of the later railway. When the TV transmitter on North Hessary Tor comes into full view, with Yellowmead Farm below, and where the track curves right again round the base of King's Tor, bear left **E** off the track and descend towards a wall corner.

Keeping the wall on the left, follow it to meet and cross a stream and continue in a straight line, making for a tall solitary stone on the horizon.

There are two such stones visible but make for the one ahead, not the one on the left. The latter is a prehistoric 'menhir', i.e. a standing stone, while the stone you are heading for **F** has a 'T' marked on one side of it and an 'A' on the other. This is an old guide-stone, erected here around 1700, to help guide travellers across the moor from Tavistock to Ashburton (hence the 'T' and 'A'). It serves as an introduction to the Merrivale Antiquities – an assortment of Bronze Age remains lying just to the left in the direction of the Dartmoor Inn and the Merrivale quarries. Of the many collections of prehistoric remains on Dartmoor, this is one of the largest and most interesting, comprising stone circles, burial chambers, groups of circular huts, standing stones and stone rows. From the extent of the remains –

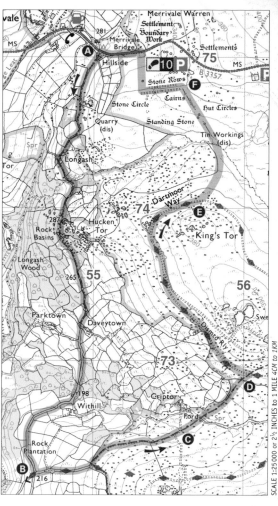

even if they are sometimes difficult to distinguish from the natural rocks which lie round about in profusion – it would appear that this was a site of some importance, a religious centre or tribal capital or perhaps both.

Bear left to find two parallel lines of stone rows. Bear left to pass between them, noting on the left the broken stone lid of a burial chamber. At the end of the rows turn right and head for the road, crossing a leat and passing (on the right) foundations of Bronze Age circular huts, before bearing right and dropping back to the car park.   ●

Widecombe in the Moor and Hamel Down

Widecombe in the Moor and Hamel Down

		GPS waypoints
Start	Widecombe in the Moor	
Distance	7 miles (11.3km)	✐ SX 719 768
Approximate time	3½ hours	**A** SX 716 769
		B SX 707 775
Parking	Widecombe in the Moor – either the car park with toilets, or the overflow one, which is on the actual route; both fee-paying	**C** SX 708 789
		D SX 704 801
		E SX 705 801
		F SX 720 802
Refreshments	Pubs and cafés at Widecombe	**G** SX 723 796
Ordnance Survey maps	Landranger 191 (Okehampton & North Dartmoor), Explorer OL28 (Dartmoor)	**H** SX 724 788

After an initial steep climb, the gradients are reasonably easy. Many of the paths along Hamel Down are not marked on the map, so follow the directions carefully. There are fine views all the way, and slight detours can be made for scrambling forays at Chinkwell Tor and Bonehill Rocks.

Famed for its fair, and even more for the song *Old Uncle Tom Cobley and All*, Widecombe is the most popular tourist centre on Dartmoor. It remains a delightful village with a splendid setting in the valley of the East Webburn, cradled amid tor-strewn moorland. It has some fine old buildings and its landmark late medieval church, often called the 'cathedral of the moor', has a 122ft (36.6m) tower.

✐ Walk across the village green and turn right to Natsworthy, passing the pub car park on the left. The footpath begins up a steep lane on the left **A**, signposted to Hamel Down and Grimspound. Where the lane bears left through a gate, keep straight ahead up a rocky track to emerge onto the down through a gate. The track bears left, then right, gently uphill, parallel to a wall on the right. Pass one signpost; keep following the wall to reach another signpost **B** by the topmost point of the wall, where it swings east. Continue

straight ahead along the left of two grassy paths that climb the hill (Two Moors Way). The craggy tors over the valley to the right will be encountered on the return leg.

The path meets a wall on the left, which runs past Hameldown Beacon cairn **C** to end at Two Barrows cairn. Head for the large earthwork – Broad Barrow – at the top of the next hill. As you approach it take the narrow path with the Two Moors Way sign skirting left around the earthwork. The stumpy remains of Hamel Down Cross **D** come into view ahead, left of the path.

From the cross strike eastwards, back over the Two Moors Way. Keep straight ahead through heather to cross one path, and ahead again to reach another broad path (Broad Barrow lies along this to the right). Turn left **E**; eventually this path sweeps right, with fine views towards Moretonhampstead ahead left. The path drops downhill past a prominent memorial stone to RAF personnel killed in a crash

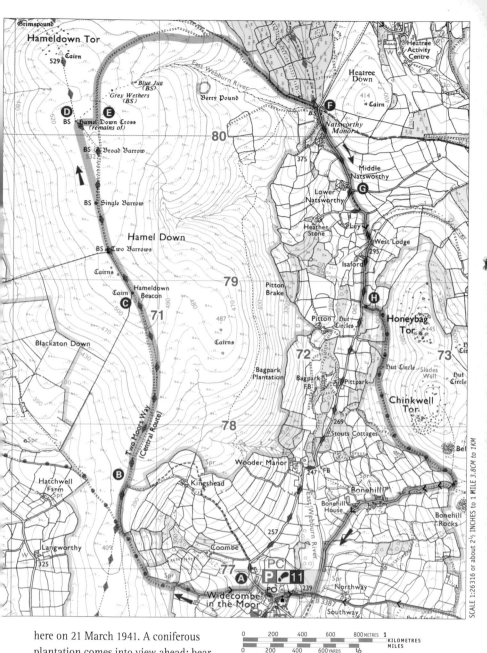

here on 21 March 1941. A coniferous plantation comes into view ahead; bear right soon after the memorial and continue downhill to reach Natsworthy Gate **F**.

Turn right along the lane; at Lower Natsworthy (where a farm track leads off left), go through the gate on the left **G** to short cut via a footpath along the left edge of the field. Rejoin the lane via a gate and turn left. Continue downhill to a cattle-grid; turn left **H** up a steep, rocky

track. This passes through a gate beneath Honeybag Tor, and continues on below Chinkwell. As it skirts Bell Tor, Widecombe comes into view. The track emerges onto the lane opposite Bonehill Rocks; turn right and descend steeply to meet the road to Widecombe. Turn right for the village centre. ●

Dartmeet, Combestone and Brimpts Wood

Start	Dartmeet	GPS waypoints	
Distance	6½ miles (10.5km). Shorter version 4 miles (6.4km)	🖊	SX 672 732
		Ⓐ	SX 669 725
Approximate time	3½ hours (1¾ hours for shorter version)	Ⓑ	SX 679 713
		Ⓒ	SX 668 718
		Ⓓ	SX 661 724
Parking	Dartmeet	Ⓔ	SX 663 730
Refreshments	Café at Dartmeet and at Brimpts Farm, tearoom at Badger's Holt	Ⓕ	SX 672 746
		Ⓖ	SX 678 750
Ordnance Survey maps	Landrangers 191 (Okehampton & North Dartmoor) and 202 (Torbay & South Dartmoor), Explorer OL28 (Dartmoor)		

This is basically a summer walk, though after heavy rain, it may prove impossible. The reason is the use of stepping stones. If the ones at Dartmeet are impassable, do not attempt this walk; but if the weather is dry, this is a delightful route with a rare mix of Dartmoor countryside. The walk can be shortened, after point Ⓔ.

🖊 Cross the bridge at Dartmeet and, by the old petrol pumps on the left, take the blue-waymarked path signed for the stepping stones. *Do not attempt this if the stones are covered.* The path climbs away from the river up through trees and into the meadow at the top. Keep the hedge or wall on your left through two fields. At lovely Combestone Farm bear left Ⓐ over the cattle-grid to a green lane beyond the farmyard. This becomes a track, with wonderful views over the West Dart. Pass through a gate into a brackeny area before dropping to cross a small stream by a stone bridge. Bear slightly left, then right uphill to find a sunken track that ascends, above the stream, to reach the road Ⓑ. Turn right along the lane for Combestone Tor.

Just as the road begins its steep descent beyond the tor, look for a farm track on the right Ⓒ. At the cattle-grid bear left on the blue-waymarked footpath to Huccaby

via Week Ford. The route is always downhill and waymarked. Eventually bear right, aiming for the valley bottom below the green sward south of Huccaby House. At the river turn left through a gate; cross a small stream, then the Dart on stepping stones Ⓓ. Follow the blue waymarks to Huccaby on a path which climbs the hill using a sunken track. This emerges onto the moor, with the river and Huccaby House on the left and Huccaby Farm ahead. Beyond the farmyard there is a choice Ⓔ: either return to Dartmeet via the gate up the track to the right, following yellow waymarks thereon, or walk down to the lane and turn right there to begin the second leg of the walk.

The lane leads up to the main Two Bridges–Dartmeet road. Turn right again, then left along the blue-waymarked track to Brimpts Farm (Dartmoor Pony Heritage Trust, farmhouse food, cream teas on

SCALE 1:26 316 or about 2½ INCHES to 1 MILE 3.8CM to 1KM

offer). The path passes behind the farmhouse, then through the farmyard and ahead through a gate. Look for a signpost pointing downhill to the right, then left along a track dropping towards the river. This delightful path leads to the wooded banks of the East Dart. Continue along the riverside path to the stepping stones **F**, which should be crossed with care. Follow the path on the other side by a stream, right, which is soon crossed by a clapper bridge. Turn left, then bear right away from the stream to reach the road, and turn right.

Just beyond Rogues Roost, take the yellow waymarked footpath over the wall on the right **G**. Keep ahead across the meadow to a gate. The next meadow is boggy: follow the path to a footbridge over a stream. Climb the hill past a vegetable plot and uphill again to a stile. The path meanders pleasantly along the eastern flank of Yar Tor before descending to reach the driveway to the Badger's Holt tearoom and the Dartmeet car park. ●

Ivybridge, the Erme valley and Western Beacon

		GPS waypoints
Start	Ivybridge. (From the town centre, follow Erme Road, which runs along the left-hand bank of the River Erme. Continue up Station Road to pass the health centre. The entrance to Ivybridge Community Woodland will be seen ahead as the road bears left, with the entrance to Arjo Wiggins paper mill on the right.)	🥾 SX 635 566 Ⓐ SX 635 568 Ⓑ SX 631 589 Ⓒ SX 630 596 Ⓓ SX 643 595 Ⓔ SX 655 593 Ⓕ SX 656 593 Ⓖ SX 654 576 Ⓗ SX 645 576
Distance	7½ miles (12.1km)	
Approximate time	4 hours	
Parking	There are spaces on Station Road and Harford Road (on the opposite side of the river)	
Refreshments	Cafés and pubs in Ivybridge	
Ordnance Survey maps	Landranger 202 (Torbay & South Dartmoor), Explorer OL28 (Dartmoor)	

A delightful walk, which early on passes beneath the viaduct of the Great Western Railway. Note that parts of the riverbank path are very boggy at all times of year; stout boots are essential. A farmland stretch culminates with a walk over open moorland to the heights of Butterdon Hill and Western Beacon, both of which are magnificent viewpoints.

🥾 A footpath leads up the Erme valley from the Ivybridge Community Woodland noticeboard.

This is the start of a delightful river-side path, but note that parts – especially beyond the Community Woodland – are muddy almost all year round: stout boots are required. Follow the tumbling Erme towards the spectacular viaduct. Just before passing it turn left over the leat. Climb steep wooden steps to pass under the viaduct and reach a track Ⓐ; turn right and continue up the left bank of the river.

At the time of writing the path through the Community Woodland was closed due to subsidence. If so, turn left at the

entrance and walk up the road to reach a gate on the right; pass through and continue under the viaduct to pick up the riverbank path.

The walk along the banks of the Erme is likely to take you the best part of an hour. Pass picnic tables on the right, after which the path rises a little from the river and crosses a ladder stile. The next section is something of a challenge, negotiating a couple of streams and old granite walls, and a couple of stiles. Very boggy stretches alternate with patches of pretty beech woodland: persevere and you'll get through. Turn sharp left away from the river at a footpath post Ⓑ, crossing

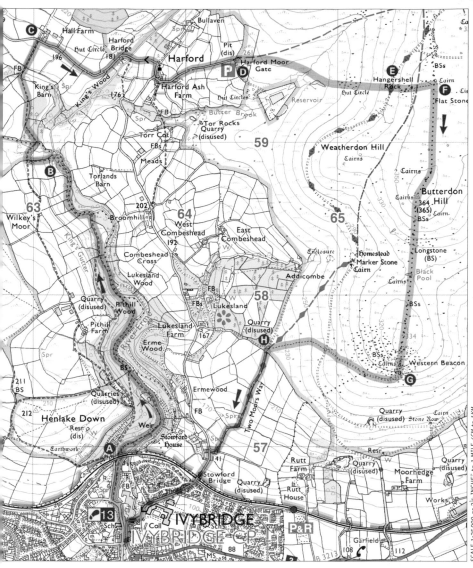

another stream; follow the path steeply uphill and over two stiles, with a fence on the right. A few yards farther on you reach a signpost with a gate to the right. Go through this and cross open ground to pass through a metal gate, and a wooden one immediately on the left, into woodland. At the top pass through a wooden gate; bear right along the field edge. Cross the next field, aiming for the left end of a wall. Drop downhill over a stream and

through a gate onto a walled track, to reach the lane opposite Hall Farm via a gate **C**. Turn right here and carry on along this lane to the village of Harford (little more than two farms and the church). The latter, dedicated to St Petroc, should not be missed. It has a beautiful interior, with slender granite columns supporting a barrel-shaped roof, and there is a famous brass and old memorial stones in the ringers' chamber, which is more or less at ground level. Leave St Petroc's Church via the lychgate and emerge onto the lane. Turn left up the steep hill to reach Harford Moor car park .

Climb the bank of the car park ahead and continue across open moorland. Look for Hangershell Rock, the prominent tor straight ahead. Descend to cross the stream immediately left of the small coniferous plantation surrounding a small reservoir. Climb the slope beyond to cross a well-made track (along which runs the Two Moors Way). From the summit of the Rock **E** continue eastwards to find a well-defined north–south path, by a cairn, following a line of indistinct boundary stones. Turn right (southwards) **F**; follow this towards Butterdon Hill. A triangulation point on this summit testifies to its excellence as a viewpoint. From Butterdon continue southwards, still following the stone row, descending to the tiny Black Pool (usually a popular meeting place for ponies), before climbing again to reach the top of Western Beacon **G**. This is the southernmost of Dartmoor's hilltops and one of its best viewpoints. Ivybridge lies below, while beyond, Plymouth Sound can be seen clearly, the sun glimmering on its waters.

Bear right and drop downhill a short distance from the summit. Turn right to pick up a small path, which broadens and drops downhill to cross a track. Continue downhill to a gate in the wall on the left **H**, where there is a sign for the Two Moors Way. Pass through and keep along the track, eventually bearing right to meet a tarmac lane. Turn left downhill towards the town. Cross Cole Lane (with modern houses right), and continue down Harford Road to pass the paper mill. Turn right over the first bridge across the river, then right up Station Road past the health centre to reach the starting point. ●

Ponies grazing at Hangershell Rock

Manaton, Hound Tor and Becka Falls

Start	Manaton		GPS waypoints
Distance	7 miles (11.3km). Shorter version 5 miles (8km)		✐ SX 749 811
			Ⓐ SX 741 804
Approximate time	4 hours (3 hours for shorter version)		Ⓑ SX 742 803
			Ⓒ SX 738 800
			Ⓓ SX 748 787
Parking	Manaton Green		Ⓔ SX 756 789
Refreshments	Pub at Manaton		Ⓕ SX 758 801
Ordnance Survey maps	Landranger 191 (Okehampton & North Dartmoor), Explorer OL28 (Dartmoor)		Ⓖ SX 767 804
			Ⓗ SX 765 810
			Ⓙ SX 759 808

This walk offers a delightful, ever-changing mix of fields, old woodland and moor with a few severe gradients but many fine viewpoints. A shorter version of the walk misses Becka Valley and Hound Tor Wood. Note that the right-of-way passes through the Becka Falls estate. This has nature trails and other facilities that are for paying customers only.

It is hard to appreciate today that peaceful Manaton, with its lovely 15th-century church situated ¹/₂ mile (800m) north west of the village, was once the centre of a tin-mining industry.

The car park is at the north-western end of Manaton, just off the road which leads to the green and the church (it is easy to overshoot this turning).

✐ On the opposite side of the main road is a lane signposted to Leighon. Take this and pass a large house on the right (Mill Farm) after crossing a stream. Walk a few yards uphill and turn right, through a gate, marked 'Hayne Road, Hayne Down and Jay's Grave'. Cross the field diagonally to a stile onto a lane. Turn right; continue uphill past a house on the right. The lane becomes a steep track through woods, leading to a gate onto Hayne Down.

Follow the bridleway uphill. Near the top take the narrow path forking right;

continue uphill to the far right edge of the jumble of granite outcrops at the top. From here Ⓐ you can look down onto the extraordinary granite column known as Bowerman's Nose. Various legends are linked to this feature; John Bowerman himself was buried in North Bovey in 1663. Turn 180 degrees (south-east) and walk ahead, with Hay Tor on the far horizon. On meeting the grassy saddle turn right Ⓑ and follow a path downhill towards a bungalow amongst conifers below left, to reach a lane. Turn left Ⓒ through Moyle's Gate and follow the lane to the junction at Swallerton Gate. Cross the lane and head towards the right edge of Hound Tor. Skirt the tor and continue downhill towards Greator Rocks. Pass through the ruined medieval village and follow the path to the left of Greator Rocks, to a gate and bridleway labelled 'Leighon and Haytor Down' Ⓓ.

The distinctive profile of Bowerman's Nose

The path descends steeply via two gates to reach a stream crossed by a stone bridge. Climb the rocky path on the other side to emerge from woodland with Smallacombe Rocks above right. At the signpost bear left to Leighon. Eventually this path passes through a gate **E** then runs between granite walls, passing through another gate to reach a track above Leighon. This soon branches; keep ahead uphill via a gate onto the shoulder of Black Hill, giving fine views of Manaton left. Bear left to meet a lane by a cattle-grid. Turn left down the lane to New Bridge *(care is needed if you have children or dogs, or both, as the lane is steep and narrow)* and at the junction with the Manaton–Bovey Tracey road turn right. Walk on the right-

hand side of the road for about 100 yds (91m) before turning left off it round a barrier with a footpath arrow. Cross the stream, and follow the path through a gate to reach a junction of paths. Take the second right (marked with a yellow arrow) which leads to a T-junction of paths **F**.

If you wish to shorten the walk, turn left. You will emerge from woodland into a meadow; keep to the left of this to reach houses near the Kestor Inn. The church is about $^{1}/_{2}$ mile (800m) along the road.

The longer route goes right at the T-junction. The right-of-way is marked by posts with yellow arrows as it winds its way through beautiful woodland. You will soon hear the sound of Becka Falls ahead of you. Stay on the path with yellow

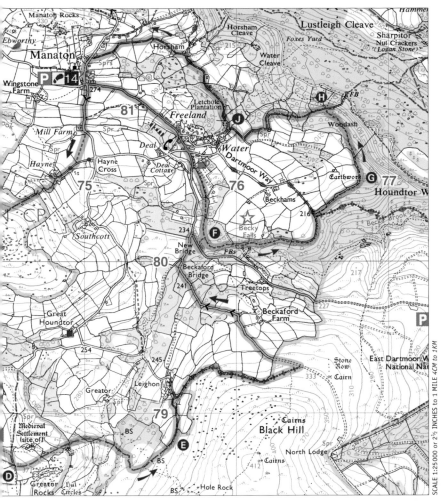

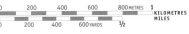

SCALE 1:25000 or 2½ INCHES to 1 MILE 4CM to 1KM

| 0 | 200 | 400 | 600 | 800 METRES | 1 |
| 0 | 200 | 400 | 600 YARDS | ½ | |

KILOMETRES
MILES

arrows, passing between animal pens and then alongside a footbridge. The land on either side is private. Keep the river on the right and continue ahead to pass a viewpoint (best when the trees are bare or in early leaf) over the falls at a memorial seat.

The path becomes steep and narrow and climbs to reach a stile at the boundary of the Becka Falls estate. On the other side, the path joins a track, which leads along the top of woodland. At a crossways keep ahead on the footpath heading for the Bovey Valley. The path immediately bears right, still keeping to the top edge of the wood.

Keep ahead to reach a fork with a footpath post; bear left **G** as signed, and after a few yards turn left again to climb to a faint path, which is marked with yellow dots on trees. The path continues to climb to an English Nature noticeboard. After this it drops down the steep side of the valley and eventually meets a bridleway **H**.

Turn left and climb to the top of the woods again (negotiating several wet sections), passing through a gate en route, to reach habitation at Water. Turn right at crossways here **J** to follow the (indirect) bridleway to Manaton. This passes through woodland, dropping downhill over a small ford. Turn left uphill; on reaching the lane turn left towards the car park. ●

Horrabridge and Sampford Spiney

Horrabridge and Sampford Spiney

		GPS waypoints	
Start	Horrabridge, by the Leaping Salmon Inn	🥾 SX 513 699	
Distance	6 miles (9.7km)	Ⓐ SX 516 704	
Approximate time	3 hours	Ⓑ SX 522 714	
Parking	Street parking in Horrabridge	Ⓒ SX 529 720	
		Ⓓ SX 533 724	
Refreshments	Pubs in Horrabridge	Ⓔ SX 536 727	
Ordnance Survey maps	Landranger 201 (Plymouth & Launceston), Explorer OL28 (Dartmoor)	Ⓕ SX 536 721	
		Ⓖ SX 529 711	
		Ⓗ SX 531 703	
		Ⓙ SX 521 696	

This walk provides an opportunity to get to know an unfrequented part of Dartmoor. There are plenty of places to shelter and the gradients are never overtaxing.

The Leaping Salmon Inn in Horrabridge is opposite the bridge, and the walk begins on the right-hand side of its car park.

🥾 The path leads into a meadow overlooking the village. Cross a stile into another field, keep ahead through a gap in the hedge, and keep ahead again to meet a farm track via a gate Ⓐ. Turn right to meet Jordan Lane. Turn left, then after a few yards turn right over a stile on the footpath to Sampford Spiney (marked yellow). Cross the field, turning left just past a ruined building, to a gate. Turn right on a green lane with a large house (Monkswell) left. Go through a metal gate into a field; keep the hedge on the left to another green lane. This leads via dilapidated gates through a partially abandoned farmyard (Monkswell Farm). Continue along a farm track, giving views ahead of Pew Tor and Sampford Spiney church, behind trees, to meet a lane.

Cross the lane Ⓑ to a waymarked stile opposite at the top of steep steps in the bank. Follow the path between beech hedges (with restored farm buildings right) into an enclosed green way. Cross the stile

into a steep-sided meadow. Keep to the top; the path soon descends towards a stream in the valley right. Cross another stream ahead, then a stile into the meadow. Follow the waymarked path, parallel to the main stream, to reach a lane via a stile. Cross the lane Ⓒ and waymarked stile onto a narrow path. Another stile leads into a field; keep the hedge on the right. Continue along the right edge of fields; three gates later Sampford Spiney village green is reached Ⓓ.

Keep ahead to pass to the left of the beautiful grey-blue church (dating from 1250) to meet a lane with broad verges. Turn left. When this bends sharp left turn right through a gate on the waymarked footpath Ⓔ, across the farmyard at Gee's Farm. Bear right to a footpath through a gateway. Cross the next two fields diagonally to a gate, overlooking Pew and Heckwood Tors. Keep the hedge on the right to the ladder stile over the bank into the next field. Continue, keeping the wall right. Pass through a gate and along the right edge of the next field, then another into an enclosed lane with a wood left.

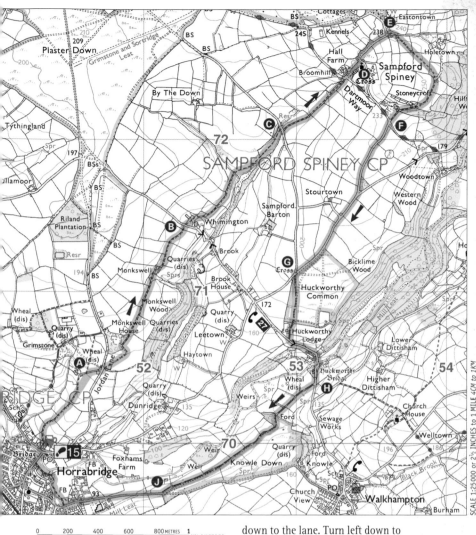

0	200	400	600	800 METRES	1
					KILOMETRES
					MILES
0	200	400	600 YARDS	½	

Continue to the road below Stoneycroft via a gate **F**. Turn left along this for just over 1 mile (1.6km) – a pleasant walk with primroses, foxgloves or blackberries according to the season. Keep right at the lane junction to emerge on the edge of Huckworthy Common.

At Huckworthy Cross **G**, by the cattle-grid, bear left across the common on a broad green path roughly parallel to the edge of the common right, before bearing half-right downhill, with Walkhampton ahead in the distance. The path descends to a gate leading to a steep stony track down to the lane. Turn left down to Huckworthy Bridge.

Some 200 yds (184m) beyond the bridge, look for a bridleway sign on the left and turn right **H** along a cart track. This leads to a delightful stream crossed by stepping stones. Bear slightly left uphill, then right on an enclosed track along the lower edge of the access land. This opens onto a bracken-covered expanse, the path eventually emerging onto the Walkhampton–Horrabridge road by a cattle-grid **J**. Turn right downhill towards Horrabridge; after ½ mile (800m) turn right on a footpath just past Tinner's Mill. This leads by playing fields to the river and back to the starting point. ●

SCALE 1:25000 or 2½ INCHES to 1 MILE 4CM to 1KM

Gidleigh, Kes Tor and Teign-e-ver Bridge

Gidleigh, Kes Tor and Teign-e-ver Bridge

		GPS waypoints	
Start	Frenchbeer Rock	🖉	SX 672 853
Distance	5½ miles (8.9km)	Ⓐ	SX 671 854
Approximate time	3 hours	Ⓑ	SX 665 862
Parking	Off the road near Frenchbeer Rock	Ⓒ	SX 660 862
Refreshments	None	Ⓓ	SX 654 873
Ordnance Survey maps	Landranger 191 (Okehampton & North Dartmoor), Explorer OL28 (Dartmoor)	Ⓔ	SX 671 882
		Ⓕ	SX 669 872
		Ⓖ	SX 670 870
		Ⓗ	SX 674 857

The route follows the Mariners' Way for much of the distance, an ancient trackway supposed to have taken its name from the sailors who, having signed off a boat in, say, Dartmouth, would then trek across the peninsula to sign on with another at Bideford.

There are places to park on the brow of the hill off the road opposite Frenchbeer Rock (reached after negotiating a labyrinth of narrow lanes).

🖉 From the road head north-west across the open ground to reach the rock, which is a wonderful viewpoint Ⓐ. To the north-east, beyond Chagford, Castle Drogo will be visible on a reasonably clear day. From the rock continue in the same direction over the moor, first to Middle Tor and then to Kestor Rock Ⓑ.

From this summit you will see Batworthy House half-hidden in trees on the left (Little Hound Tor appears beyond the house in the distance). Make for the far left-hand corner of the grounds (Batworthy Corner) Ⓒ and keep the wall right down to the North Teign River. Just left (up river) are three clapper bridges: the North Teign, Teign-e-ver and Wallabrook. The North Teign clapper bridge was reinstated in 1999. It is a magical place to pause and take in the sheer space of Dartmoor.

Keeping near the wall on the right descend to cross narrow Teign-e-ver

Bridge onto an island formed where the river divides. Bear left and leave the island by another clapper bridge and make for Scorhill Circle, walking first ahead uphill and later bearing left to reach the prehistoric circle Ⓓ (unique on Dartmoor in that it has never been restored). Take the meandering track to the right of the monument, gently uphill, then descend through a broad-mouthed newtake to follow a wall on the left and leave the moor via a wooden gate at Scorhill Farm. Follow the lane downhill. Bear right at the lane junction to the hamlet of Berrydown and then continue for about ½ mile (800m), until a yellow-waymarked sign-post pointing to the Mariners' Way appears on the right Ⓔ, after a block of trees.

Follow the wide main track; be careful not to miss the signpost at the first clearing. Bear half-right here along a lovely path that threads through bluebells and begins to descend steeply, looking as though it will disappear into a gloomy tunnel as it goes down. When it reaches a broad track above the river, follow it until

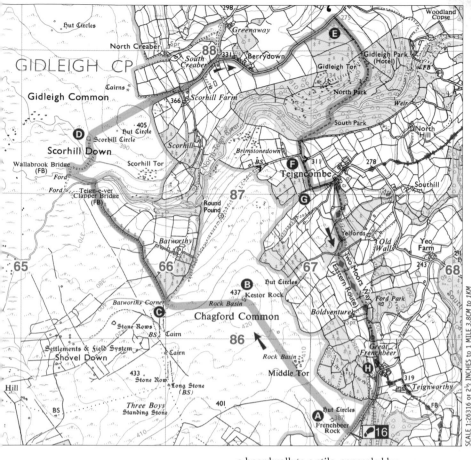

SCALE 1:26316 or 2½ INCHES to 1 MILE 3.8CM to 1KM

0	200	400	600	800 METRES	1
					KILOMETRES
					MILES
0	200	400	600 YARDS	½	

you find a signpost turning left to the footbridge; cross it and climb a steep path to reach a broad track at the top. Turn left at the metalled road and, after 20 yds (18m) turn right **F**, following the Mariners' Way towards Frenchbeer.

At first there is a charming, level section rich in wild flowers but, at a T-junction **G** the way lies to the left, downhill over slippery rocks. At the bottom of this path, by the Mariners' Way timber house, keep ahead through a gate as signed. Pass almost immediately through another gate to enter a long meadow. Keep the hedge right and climb to the top right-hand corner of the field, cross a stile, then a small footbridge. Walk through the next field, then along

a boardwalk to a stile, concealed by rhododendrons. Next comes a short walk through a new plantation. Go over a stile and straight across a field, keeping the hedge left. Pass through a wooden gate on the far side. A boggy stretch through woodland is traversed via a boardwalk. Climb a stile to cross a small meadow, and another stile and over a track; cross a stile into the next meadow. Go over a stile and through a brackeny area, with conifers left, and over another stile. The path breaks out into open country with views south and east. Pass through a wooden gate, after which a short section of enclosed path leads to the thatched farmhouse of Frenchbeer, where you leave the Mariners' Way to turn right **H** up the steep, metalled road. This levels out beyond the cattle-grid, and a short distance on is the open moor and starting point. ●

Okehampton, Cullever Steps and Belstone (vertical side text)

Okehampton, Cullever Steps and Belstone

		GPS waypoints
Start	Okehampton	
Distance	7½ miles (12.1km)	🏁 SX 587 951
Approximate time	4½ hours	Ⓐ SX 585 944
		Ⓑ SX 587 943
Parking	Okehampton	Ⓒ SX 593 939
Refreshments	Pubs and cafés at Okehampton, pub at Belstone	Ⓓ SX 603 930
		Ⓔ SX 605 921
Ordnance Survey maps	Landranger 191 (Okehampton & North Dartmoor), Explorer OL28 (Dartmoor)	Ⓕ SX 610 916
		Ⓖ SX 617 914
		Ⓗ SX 618 935
		Ⓙ SX 612 942
		Ⓚ SX 603 948

The northern part of Dartmoor contains not only the highest land in southern England but also some of the wildest and loneliest; bleak, even featureless, it is nonetheless impressive in its austere and sweeping emptiness. The walk ventures into the fringes of this wilderness, which, considered eminently suitable for military training purposes, has been used for this by the army since the 1870s. Although this walk passes close to the firing ranges, it does not actually enter any of them. Because of the nature of much of the terrain, it is advisable not to attempt this walk in poor weather and misty conditions, unless you are an experienced walker, able to use a compass.

Okehampton lies on the northern edge of Dartmoor, astride one of the main routes between Exeter and Cornwall. To the south lies the wildest part of the moor, to the north is the much gentler, rolling, wooded countryside of mid Devon. Its fine Town Hall was originally a private house, built in 1685 and converted to serve the purposes of local government in the early 19th century.

🖉 The walk begins in the main street (Fore Street). Turn down George Street, and then bear right along Castle Road, following signs to Okehampton Castle. Just before the bridge over the West Okement River, keep ahead, entering hospital grounds, along a fenced path between the river and old hospital buildings. Past the end of the buildings continue along the riverside path, go through a kissing-gate and head towards the woods in front.

A short detour over a footbridge on the right Ⓐ leads up to the entrance to Okehampton Castle. The castle was founded soon after the Norman Conquest and throughout the Middle Ages; it was one of the principal fortresses in the West Country, owned for much of its history by the powerful Courtenay family, earls of Devon. Today its romantic-looking ruins, mostly comprising the 12th-century keep

The romantic ruins of Okehampton Castle

and 14th-century domestic buildings and chapel, occupy a fine site above the West Okement River.

Retrace your steps over the footbridge and turn half-right to regain the main route, signed West Devon Way and Meldon Viaduct. The path now climbs gently through most attractive woodland, with striking views of the castle ruins between the trees on the right. At a path junction take the left-hand fork, continuing uphill to join a narrow tarmac lane. Turn sharp left along this lane; just past the end of a wall on the right, bear slightly right along a path that keeps roughly parallel with and rises above the lane. Continue to reach a kissing-gate leading onto a road **B**.

Turn right to cross a railway bridge; continue over the Okehampton bypass.

Follow the road steadily uphill, over a cattle-grid, and round a sharp right-hand bend. At the end of a wall on the left, turn left **C** over grass and left again through a gate by a cattle-grid, at public footpath and public bridleway signs. Walk along a farm road from where there are extensive and greatly contrasting views: to the left over Okehampton, lying below, and the farmlands of mid Devon beyond, and to the right over open moorland, with the Okehampton army camp clearly visible.

The immediate area was once part of Okehampton Park, the hunting ground adjoining the castle; although it is still attractive, its previously unspoilt beauty has now been affected both by the presence of the army and by the construction of the Okehampton bypass.

Follow the farm road through Lower Halstock Farm. Do not go through the signed gate ahead but follow the track as it bears right uphill to pass through a gate. Continue uphill through gates and gateways to reach open moorland via a gate just past buildings left **D**. Keep by a wall on the left, bearing slightly left at the end of it. Keep straight ahead, following a track due south (almost immediately crossing another) which soon heads down towards the East Okement river below on the left. Ahead of you are most impressive views of wild, bleak, rocky moorland, the hilltops studded with granite tors. Among these hills are Yes Tor and High Willhays, both over 610m (2,000ft), the highest points in southern England.

At Cullever Steps **E**, the site of an ancient ford, cross the footbridges and keep ahead to a junction of tracks. Turn right, almost immediately bearing left to follow a track that zigzags up the side of the hill. After 100 yds (92m) bear left uphill towards the line of a ruined wall ahead on the slopes of Belstone Tor.

This is the Irishman's Wall, apparently built by a group of Irishmen in the 19th century as part of a scheme by a land speculator to enclose areas of the moor; it was pulled down by the locals as fast as it was put up.

Rejoin the track and keep ahead, soon bearing right along it in a southerly direction. At Winter Tor (right) turn left **F** and ascend towards the right (lower) edge of Higher Tor, with excellent views across the Taw Plain to Cosdon Hill, with Steeperton Tor at the head of the valley.

Descend to a track opposite a ford **G**, turn left and follow it for ¾ mile (1.2km) to a gate by the first group of trees seen for quite a while. Go through, keep ahead along a tarmac track, passing a cottage on the right, and bear right, past more cottages, straight ahead for another ¼ mile (400m) to the village of Belstone, standing 315m (1,020ft) up on the edge of Dartmoor between the Taw and East Okement rivers.

Approaching the village bear left at a junction, passing the pub on the left (the small, simple, heavily restored 13th-century church lies behind), then left again at a T-junction and almost immediately turn half-right **H**. Keep along this lane for ¾ mile (1.2km) and, just past a cattle-grid, turn left **J** over a stile at a public footpath sign to Fatherford. Head straight across a field, through a gap by a public footpath sign, and continue along the edge of the next field by a wall and line of trees on the right. Climb a stile, walk along the edge of a field, this time with a line of trees on the left, heading downhill to climb another stile. Continue along the edge of the next field down to a stream, cross a footbridge and keep ahead for a few yards to go through a wooden gate.

Turn left along a lane to pass under the bypass and a railway. Just beyond the railway bridge, turn left along a lane, and immediately left again **K**. At a footpath sign turn right through a gate and along a narrow path through Ball Hill conservation area, soon joining the East Okement river. Keep either by or above it along a most

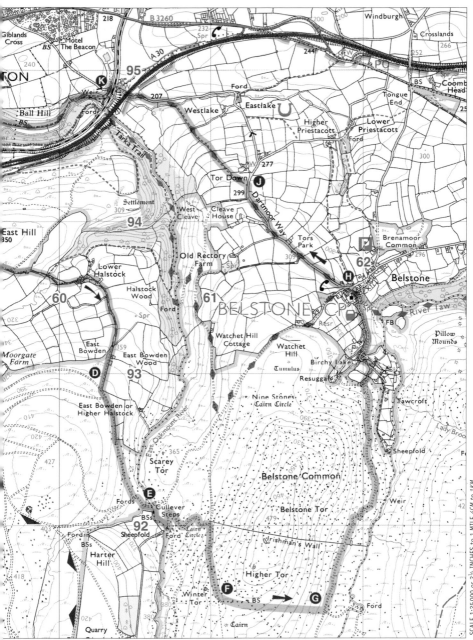

attractive path that climbs through the thick woods of Ball Hill and drops down again, continuing to a gate.

Pass through, keep straight ahead to a gate, go through that and keep along the edge of a field to go through another gate. Continue along a well-surfaced path to pass through yet another gate. Keep by a stream on the left and pass through a wooden gate and along a tarmac lane, now with the stream right and part of Okehampton College left. On the left is a former mill building; turn left down some steps by the side of it and then bear left along the road ahead, following it as it curves right over the river and continuing ahead for a short distance back to Okehampton town centre. ●

South Zeal and Little Hound Tor

Start	Newlyn Cottage, on the old A30 at South Zeal		**GPS waypoints**
Distance	6 miles (9.7km)		🥾 SX 648 932
Approximate time	3½ hours		Ⓐ SX 645 931
Parking	Lay-by just north of Newlyn Cottage on the old A30, or public car park in South Zeal		Ⓑ SX 646 918
			Ⓒ SX 644 915
			Ⓓ SX 638 903
Refreshments	Pubs in South Zeal		Ⓔ SX 632 896
Ordnance Survey maps	Landranger 191 (Okehampton & North Dartmoor), Explorer OL28 (Dartmoor)		Ⓕ SX 632 896
			Ⓖ SX 626 906
			Ⓗ SX 625 907
			Ⓙ SX 628 914
			Ⓚ SX 627 924
			Ⓛ SX 643 930

This moorland walk is for fair weather only and requires good map-reading skills, as it goes into the heart of some of Dartmoor's wildest countryside. It passes two of Dartmoor's most interesting Bronze Age monuments: White Moor stone circle and 'The Graveyard' which is a triple-line stone row 447ft (136m) long. South Zeal is one of the most picturesque of Dartmoor villages. (The word 'village' however, is something of a misnomer, as South Zeal was in fact granted the status of borough in 1299.) Its first bypass (the old A30) was built for the coaching road in 1829.

There is a lay-by on the old A30 close to the starting point, or you may use a car park at the eastern end of the village. (From the car park, turn right; follow the lane as it bears right, eventually climbing uphill to meet the old main road by Newlyn.)

🥾 Cross the road and take the blue-waymarked bridleway by the cottage marked 'To the Moor'.

The track climbs steeply. On a right bend bear left on a path to rejoin the lane; bear right to a fork Ⓐ. Take the left fork and continue climbing up an enclosed lane. This was a route forged by peat merchants bringing peat to South Zeal

from the remote diggings on Hanging-stone Hill, far to the south.

Continue past the sign to 'Pixies' Garden' on the footpath to Cawsand and the moor. Another footpath leads to the left down to the A30. Carry straight on through a gate, and continue uphill to pass through another. A stream now shares the track, which can make the going difficult. Just as you think that this old track has at last led you onto the moor, yet another stone wall appears to enclose the track again. At least it is now dry and grassy.

When the wall on the left ends Ⓑ, bear right to find a faint banked track. Follow this, eventually passing to the left of a

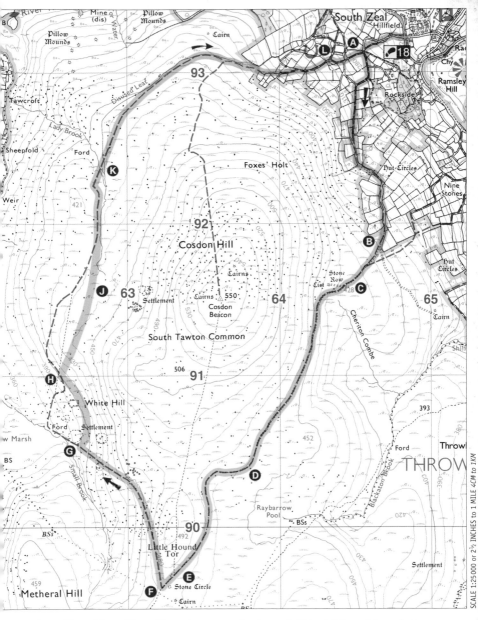

0	200	400	600	800 METRES	1	
						KILOMETRES
						MILES
0	200	400	600 YARDS		½	

Bronze Age stone row, locally known as 'The Graveyard' **C**. At the far end are the remains of a cist and retaining circle – the last resting place of a chieftain, or person of similar status. You can see the track ahead, curving left along the contours of the hill. Follow the track on, at first between banks. It becomes increasingly boggy and skirts sinister patches of mire; the original peat-cutters' track disappears in places. Ahead and left is Raybarrow Pool, one of Dartmoor's most notorious mires. A very wet patch is encountered **D**; if possible keep to the left of the banked track and follow it ahead, soon bearing right uphill. If the ground is too wet bear right uphill just before the wet section to find drier ground, soon picking up the track. It then bears left along the contours of the hill again. Quite suddenly Little Hound (or, more correctly, Round Tor) comes into view, with, below it, White Moor stone circle **E**.

From the circle return to the sunken track and walk towards Round Tor. A few yards along – where the banks along the track end – turn right **F** on a faint path leading off at right angles to the track. (This should not be confused with the more distinct track coming down from Little Hound Tor and leading, in the other direction, to the summit of Cosdon – an acute right turn.) You are now facing a grand array of high tors: Belstone Tor is the one on the extreme right. As you follow the winding path through the heather this is the one to head for. Keep well up the valley side; although the way crosses some wet patches, it is boggier further downhill. Eventually descend towards Small Brook ford below left to find the circular remains of a settlement

G. Do not go down to the ford but keep ahead, still in line with Belstone Tor. After about 200 yds (183m) bear right **H** on a faint grassy path that runs uphill towards a saddle to the left of Cosdon Hill. This becomes more distinct and levels before entering a broad gully, the source of Lady Brook. Bear left on a sunken track **J**.

The track leads eventually to the ford over Lady Brook **K** and continues on the other side. You will now have Belstone Tor directly behind you. This leg seems a long way but the tower of South Tawton church appears ahead at last and then, as a rough cart track appears, South Zeal appears below. Keep ahead along the track, which descends, with a wall left, to leave the moor between granite walls. Pass through a gate, turn right **L** ('A30 South Zeal') and then right again at the next junction, as signed, to follow the track to the starting point. ●

The stone circle below Little Hound Tor

Postbridge, Laughter Hole and Bellever

		GPS waypoints
Start	Postbridge	
Distance	7½ miles (12.1km)	✏ SX 647 788
Approximate time	4 hours	Ⓐ SX 668 784
		Ⓑ SX 674 785
Parking	Postbridge	Ⓒ SX 676 772
Refreshments	Pub/hotel and post office (take	Ⓓ SX 681 762
	away food) at Postbridge	Ⓔ SX 679 749
Ordnance Survey maps	Landranger 191 (Okehampton &	Ⓕ SX 672 751
	North Dartmoor), Explorer OL28	Ⓖ SX 662 757
	(Dartmoor)	Ⓗ SX 655 769

This is an ideal walk for children, with plenty of interest en route and, towards the end, the chance of getting thoroughly wet in the East Dart River at Bellever. With stretches of moorland, a lovely riverside section at the start and finish, and exciting stepping stones at Laughter Hole, it also makes an excellent introduction to walking on Dartmoor.

✏ From Postbridge car park turn left to cross the bridge and take the lane on the right to Lydgate House Hotel. A pleasant alternative is to cross the clapper bridge and follow the left bank of the stream through the meadows on a

Meadows by the East Dart at Postbridge

'permitted path'; this path joins with the other just before the hotel driveway. The route, a blue way-marked bridleway, passes in front of the hotel and crosses a series of riverside meadows before bending left away from the river through a gate. Climb uphill through gorse; turn right at the wall at the top and walk along

the field edge. Pass through a gate onto a track (muddy all year round). This bears right and goes through a gate. Here the track becomes a stream-bed, so follow the right-hand side of the stream to a small stone clapper-bridge marked by a blue-topped post. Bear left at the next signpost, pass through a gate and continue uphill, following the track as it bears left through another gate to reach Pizwell.

The track bears right and runs between cottages. On reaching a T-junction of tracks **Ⓐ** keep ahead along a rough track to cross the stream via stepping stones to reach a level, heather-banked track. At a crossroads (just before Ephraim's Pinch – conifers ahead left) turn right **Ⓑ** through a gate onto a bridleway across Cator Common. About 200 yds (183m) from a belt of trees ahead, follow the marked path which bears right through a lonely gate, to reach a road via a gate **Ⓒ**. Turn left and continue for about 1 mile (1.6km), with views of Yar Tor right. Ignore the left turn at Cator Green; follow the lane onto open moor. About 50 yds (46m) later, turn right **Ⓓ** along a farm track. After 20 yds (18m) head diagonally left. This path provides wonderful views to the right over Wild Goose Farm and later ahead to Bellever Forest. On a sunny late summer's day, the heather and gorse give off an incense-like fragrance. Eventually bear left and climb to a signpost on a wall corner. Bear right as signed, with the wall right; Yar Tor now lies ahead left. The path descends to reach the road at Sherwell ('Sherrill' on some signposts) **Ⓔ**.

Turn right and follow the lane down past Rogues Roost to Babeny. Just before the farm **Ⓕ** turn right up a blue waymarked concrete track. This bears left; keep ahead on a rough waymarked path that rises behind the house. Keep parallel to and later hug the wall on the left, and follow this to a gate onto open moor. Keep ahead, then descend towards Laughter Hole House (more correctly Loughton

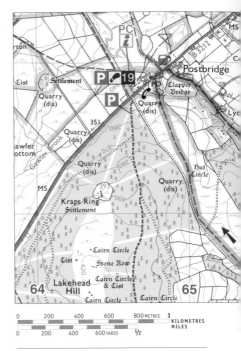

Hole). Cross the East Dart by the stepping stones **Ⓖ** and climb past the house through gates on a narrow path which then bears right through trees to meet a track. Turn right through a gate to Laughter Hole Farm and follow signs to Bellever through the farmyard, along a farm track, and eventually into the forest. Where the track bears sharp left keep ahead as signed through a small gate **Ⓗ**. Keep ahead through the Forestry Commission riverside picnic area.

The track emerges onto a lane. Cross over and head diagonally left (marked with a bridlepath arrow) for a field gate to the left of a wall, then through another onto a lane. Turn right and walk uphill on a bridlepath to the right of the lane. At the top of the hill, where a track leads away right, bear half-right on a grassy path that descends towards the river. Where the path bears left at the bottom of the hill bear right on a narrow path that drops through gorse to a gate. Pass through and keep ahead to meet the road by the clapper bridge. Turn left for the car park. ●

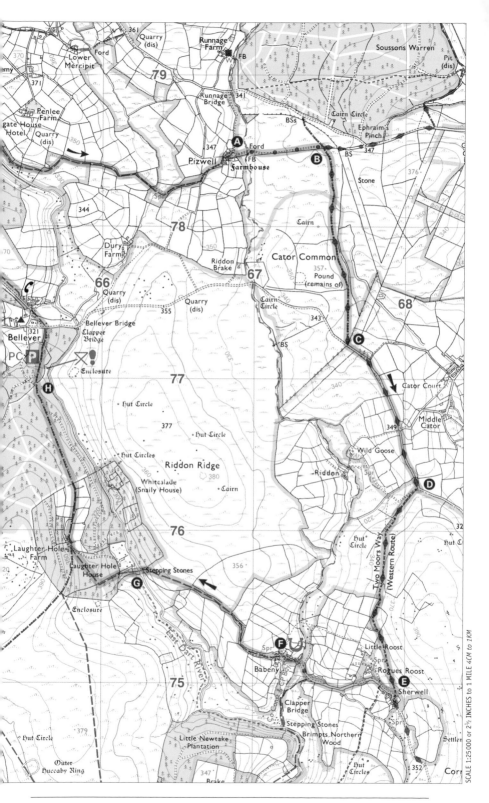

Drewsteignton, Hittisleigh Barton and Crockernwell

		GPS waypoints
Start	Drewsteignton	☑ SX 735 908
Distance	8 miles (12.9km)	Ⓐ SX 736 915
Approximate time	4 hours	Ⓑ SX 734 926
Parking	Drewsteignton	Ⓒ SX 732 937
Refreshments	Pub and cream teas in Drewsteignton	Ⓓ SX 732 950
		Ⓔ SX 734 954
Ordnance Survey maps	Landranger 191 (Okehampton & North Dartmoor), Explorer OL28 (Dartmoor)	Ⓕ SX 736 949
		Ⓖ SX 749 935
		Ⓗ SX 753 924
		Ⓙ SX 762 912
		Ⓚ SX 751 910

This is an 'alternative' walk, away from the open moors and deep into the countryside of mid Devon. Certainly you are unlikely to meet other walkers on these paths, unless they are clutching the same guidebook (or tackling the Two Moors Way). There is much to admire on these forgotten byways, which seem to lead through an unspoilt, almost timeless landscape.

With its thatched cottages and old church, Drewsteignton is one of the most charming of Dartmoor villages, situated on the northern fringes of the National Park. The walk starts from the village square, outside the Drewe Arms.

☑ Turn right from the post office and take the road to Crockernwell. Go down the hill past Netherton House, and at the Veet Mill sign carry straight on downhill, leaving the Crockernwell road. At the bottom, look for a yellow-waymarked Two Moors Way path to the A30 on the left Ⓐ. The path runs to the right of lovely, thatched Veet Mill, and then crosses the mill stream by a footbridge. Beyond the house the path widens into an ancient trackway as it accompanies the stream up the hill. After a stile and a footbridge, the track reaches Winscombe. Bear to the left to pass the farm on a concrete track as the noise of traffic from the A30 grows louder.

Follow signs left to cross the bridge, then turn right Ⓑ and, at a gateway on the left, climb the stile and follow the footpath sign. Keep the hedge on the left and make for a stile by an old Nissen hut. Keep in the same direction ahead to descend the hill, still with the hedge, heavy with blackberries and sloes in season, on the left. West Ford, the eventual destination of this footpath, can be seen in the distance. Cross two stiles, then walk diagonally across the field to reach another in the hedge close to the wood right. Cut right cross the corner of the next field to find a stile into the wood. Cross a footbridge; follow the narrow path left through the trees, with a stream left, to emerge close to West Ford. Cross the ford (or use the footbridge) and climb 20 yds (18m) up the lane to find another lane on the right. Turn right Ⓒ; immediately look for a farm track on the left. Cross the stile in the hedge to the right of this track, still on the Two Moors Way. Go through a

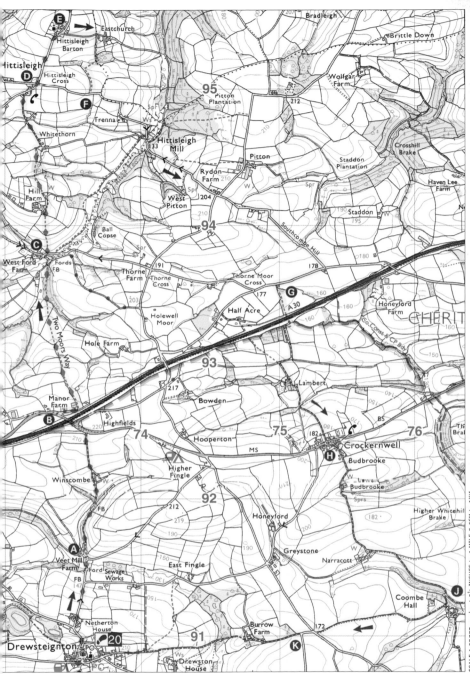

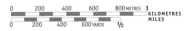

gate; turn left steeply uphill, keeping the fence left, to another stile. Continue climbing straight ahead to find a stile at the top. Keep ahead, with hedge and farmhouse left, to reach a track via another stile. Turn right, bearing left where the track forks, to reach an open gateway. Keep ahead down the field to find a stile onto an enclosed path at the bottom. Continue uphill and over a stile onto a boardwalk, ending at another stile into a field. Follow waymarks ahead then turn right over a stile into Whitethorn Farm. Turn left into the lane, and right at the next junction, to reach Hittisleigh Cross **D**.

Keep ahead, still on the Two Moors Way, for $\frac{1}{4}$ mile (400m) to reach Hittisleigh Barton church on the left. (The Two Moors Way continues ahead to eventually reach the north coast at Lynmouth.) Just past the turning to the church turn right **E** onto a narrow tarmac track. Follow this to pass through a metal gate; immediately turn right as signed, downhill along the right edge of a field. Pass through a wood and over a footbridge. Continue diagonally right uphill across a field corner; turn left along the top right edge, passing through a gate onto a lane **F**. Turn left downhill to pass Hittisleigh Mill.

From the mill, follow the lane up the steep hill and straight over the crossroads to descend Southcombe Hill. Climb the other side and turn right at the road junction. At the end of a long field on the left, look for a gate **G** on the left into a field. Keep the hedge on the right and continue under the A30. On the other side bear right through a gate into a wood. Follow the green lane left uphill, following signs right and then left to reach Lambert. Carry on down the hill and up the other side to reach Crockernwell **H**. Cross the road to the lane opposite – Stonelands – and follow this left to find a

footpath labelled 'Nr Upperton via Coombe Hall' on the right.

This leads down past thatched Lower Budbrooke. Beyond here the green lane becomes quite muddy and unkempt. Persevere and you will reach Narracott, enjoying a lovely panorama of rolling green countryside. Bear left at Narracott, keeping the hedge on the left and continuing along the top of the field. Another footpath sign, some 200 yds (183m) distant, points right down the side of a steep valley. This continues to an amazing example of a lost Devon road – gnarled oaks darken a sunken trackway, and one can almost imagine hobbits watching quietly from the twisted tree-roots. This track descends to the stream by Coombe Hall, and over a stile. Turn right to cross the stream, then follow the blue-way-marked bridleway through a gate to reach a path junction **J**. Keep ahead along the track that runs through the field in front of the hall, passing through two gates. Continue along a rough drive through the next field, uphill, to a metalled track.

After $\frac{1}{2}$ mile (800m) this meets a lane: cross over and take the way to Fingle Bridge and Drewsteignton. Almost immediately this lane bends sharply to the left. Here keep straight on **K** down the concreted track. Pass Burrough Farm on the right, and keep ahead through a waymarked gate to the right of a barn. Follow the fence, then hedge, on the right, downhill to a gate leading into a patch

Drewsteignton

of woodland and over an old packhorse bridge. On the far side of the wood go straight through a gate. Keeping the hedge on the right, continue up a steep hill, passing through two stiles and a small gate, after which the hedge is on the left. Go through a gate onto a green lane, which leads back to Drewsteignton. Continue through the churchyard to the village square. ●

Moretonhampstead, Butterdon Down and North Bovey

		GPS waypoints
Start	Moretonhampstead	🖉 SX 753 860
Distance	8½ miles (13.7km) or two separate walks of 4½ miles (7.3km) and 4 miles (6.4km)	Ⓐ SX 750 869 Ⓑ SX 748 881
Approximate time	4½ hours (2½ hours and 2 hours for the two separate walks)	Ⓒ SX 745 888 Ⓓ SX 739 890 Ⓔ SX 754 885
Parking	Moretonhampstead	Ⓕ SX 754 878
Refreshments	Pubs and cafés at Moretonhampstead, pub at North Bovey	Ⓖ SX 755 862 Ⓗ SX 753 849 Ⓙ SX 752 842
Ordnance Survey maps	Landranger 191 (Okehampton & North Dartmoor), Explorer OL28 (Dartmoor)	Ⓚ SX 745 637 Ⓛ SX 739 843 Ⓜ SX 739 849 Ⓝ SX 745 856

This is a figure of eight based on Moretonhampstead. The northern loop takes in the prehistoric remains of Cranbrook Castle, a wonderful viewpoint, and the southern loop visits the picturesque village of North Bovey. Gradients are undemanding – except for an uphill climb to Ⓐ – and the going relatively easy, although the fields encountered just after Ⓜ can be very muddy after wet weather.

Moretonhampstead lies near the eastern edge of Dartmoor. It is an attractive little town with old cottages, some fine 17th-century colonnaded almshouses and a parish church with an imposing 15th-century tower.

🖉 From the town centre take the Okehampton road (A382). Pass the road to the health centre, and turn right at a sign to Howton. Ignore the left fork to Howton, and follow the narrow lane steeply uphill. Where the lane bears suddenly to the right, look for a field gate and stile on the left Ⓐ (the sign reads 'To Fingle Bridge via Butterdon'). Cross the field diagonally and climb a stile into the next, keeping close to a wall on the left. Cross two more stiles, then look for a wooden stile in the corner of the field, with conifers along the fence to the right. Cross this stile, then a stone stile onto a lane. Go straight over, across another stile, signed Cranbrook. Follow this path along the edge of woodland, and over a stile into a field.

Now head towards Bowden Farm below, keeping the hedge on the left. Go over another stile, then cross a boggy stream on vague stepping stones. Climb the next stile, and continue uphill, keeping the hedgebank on the left, to another stile in the top corner of the next field. Keep ahead uphill to find a final stile leading onto open moorland **B**, with the bridleway to 'Near Butterdon' signed right. Bear left along the signed bridlepath (ignore the next bridlepath signed left). Continue north over Butterdown Down towards Cranbrook, passing a standing stone on the right as you head for a double stile and footpath sign on the left. After this make for a wooden stile by a wooden gate at the bottom of the field. Carry straight on with the wall left, pass through a gateway, and continue downhill to cross a stile by a gate to reach the lane at Cranbrook Cottage **C**; turn left.

Ignore the first footpath on the right to Fingle Bridge. Another five minutes of walking up the lane brings you to a track which again leads off to the right. Take this, and then fork left where signed to enter the common and walk uphill to reach the ramparts of Cranbrook Castle **D**, a vast stronghold overlooking the Teign gorge, mirrored by Prestonbury fort on the other side. Their exact date is uncertain, the earliest suggestion being around 2000BC. If this is correct, they pre-date by 3,900 years the impressive Castle Drogo, whose walls seem to rise sheer from the gorge itself.

Return to the lane and retrace the route to Cranbrook Cottage. Continue along the lane ignoring the fork to the left. You will find a footpath over a stile on the right **E** (just before the lane bends sharp left) into a wooded area. Emerge from the wood over a stile onto a narrow path between steep banks. The Butterdon footpath rejoins from the right. Turn left downhill to reach a lane junction. Keep straight on, signed Moretonhampstead. When the lane bends sharply right, keep ahead **F** down a farm track. Bear left by cottages at Hill Farm, on a steep woodland path that eventually passes through a gate and runs beside a stream. Follow the path through a more open area; it bears right, away from the stream, into woods. Go through a gate into a meadow above thatched Coombe

Court Farm below left.

Walk along the lower edge of the meadow. Go through a gate at the corner to reach a footpath junction. Go through the next gate, and then take the left (lower) path (signed Millbrook Bridge) down to the lower left-hand corner of the field. Follow the path along the bottom of the valley. Bear left to go through a gate just past the old swimming pool. Cross the stream via a footbridge and stile, and turn right along the bottom of the next field. The path emerges through a gate onto the Mardon lane by the town sign **G**. Turn right uphill to the town centre.

Here start the second leg by taking the Postbridge road, almost immediately branching left by a newsagent's shop into Pound Street. Bear left when the North Bovey road swings right, and continue down a lane. This crosses a stream, then narrows and climbs steeply. After the driveway to Brinning on the right, look for a gate and stile on the left **H**.

Follow the path over a stream and along the left edge of a meadow. There is a steep climb to a stile at the top; cross the next stile onto a farm track. Go through the kissing-gate, and cross two more stiles, to reach Narramore farm (left). Cross the field diagonally right and cross a stile to reach the drive, leading to a lane. Cross over and through a gate onto the footpath opposite (farm track). On approaching Fursdon **J**, cross the stile on the right. Cut straight across the field and across the farm drive. Go through a gate and strike left to the stile ahead. Cross the next field and leave through the gateway. Cross the following field diagonally to a stile and stream in the bottom corner. Continue straight over the next field, over a stile, and along the left edge of the next field. A stile leads to a track, which descends to meet a byway over a stile **K**. Turn right to pass the ford at North Bovey.

Go through a gate and continue uphill,

passing the green on your left. Bear right on meeting the road. At Pound Rock bear left **L**. Just before the road bears left towards a white bungalow, turn right on a footpath over a stile into a field. Cross this diagonally to a stile in the left-hand hedge and continue diagonally across the next field. Pass through two metal gates in the top corner. Turn immediately left through a wooden gate and walk diagonally across the field, and over a stile onto a metalled lane **M**. Turn right, then left into a green lane. Pass through a gate and continue through fields, keeping the hedge left. Cross a stile in the next hedge, and keep straight ahead through a metal gate, with Moretonhampstead in view. Still keeping the hedge on the left, walk down the next field and through a metal gate to reach a farm drive.

Turn left, then right through a gate opposite stables. Cross the field to a gate. Keep the hedge on the right as you descend the hill. A double stile in the right-hand corner of the field by the stream **N**, is followed by a narrow path. This crosses a stream and climbs uphill enclosed by ancient, steep banks – to reach the road.

Turn right, back to Moretonhampstead and the starting point.

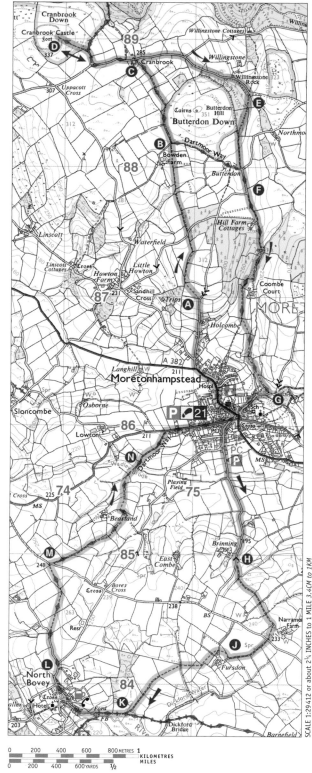

SCALE 1:29 412 or about 2½ INCHES to 1 MILE 3.4CM to 1KM

Mary Tavy, Horndon Down and Peter Tavy

Start	Mary Tavy
Distance	7 miles (11.3km)
Approximate time	4 hours
Parking	Roadside parking near church in Mary Tavy
Refreshments	Pubs at Peter Tavy and Horndon (off route)
Ordnance Survey maps	Landrangers 191 (Okehampton & North Dartmoor) and 201 (Plymouth & Launceston), Explorer OL28 (Dartmoor)

GPS waypoints

- 🔏 SX 508 787
- Ⓐ SX 505 794
- Ⓑ SX 513 807
- Ⓒ SX 522 811
- Ⓓ SX 526 807
- Ⓔ SX 531 803
- Ⓕ SX 525 794
- Ⓖ SX 523 787
- Ⓗ SX 526 780
- Ⓙ SX 518 776

A more energetic walk than you might expect, yet immensely enjoyable. The old vertical iron ladder at Hill Bridge has been superseded by wooden steps, providing easier access to the path beside the leat (water channel) that runs from the bridge through pretty Creason Wood – one of the best sections of the route.

The church at Mary Tavy is slightly less interesting inside than that of Peter Tavy, but nonetheless worth a look.

🔏 Face the church and turn left along the lane, passing the telephone box. Bear right on the lane signposted to Horndon; ignore the second turn to Horndon (opposite the school) and keep straight on downhill to the bridge, which has a white cottage standing close by it. The footpath begins on the right by the cottage Ⓐ and soon crosses the stream by a footbridge. Climb the hillside, and at the footpath sign turn left across the field to a yellow waymarked stile. The path runs parallel to a stream away to the left through a run of meadows (where there is evidence of copper mining, which took place here long ago), crossing four stiles en route. After the fourth stile keep left of a telegraph pole, with a wire fence right (this section is boggy in wet weather). Cross a

bank via stone steps onto a lane; turn left. This lane becomes a farm track at Kingsett (on the right), and climbs steadily. Go through the gate at the top end of the track Ⓑ onto the moor, keeping the wall on the right. The engine house of Wheal Betsy – where both lead and silver were mined – can be seen below the main road to the left. Crest the top of the hill, with good views ahead towards Ger Tor and Hare Tor. Follow the wall as it curves to the right and the ugly square pumping house of the Wheal Jewell Reservoir comes into view ahead left.

At a wall corner keep straight ahead downhill to pass below the southern end of the reservoir to join a track coming from it. Turn right here Ⓒ (initially between walls) with a lovely view of Cudlipptown Down ahead. Turn left onto a metalled road and then, at the end of the farm wall, immediately right down a short

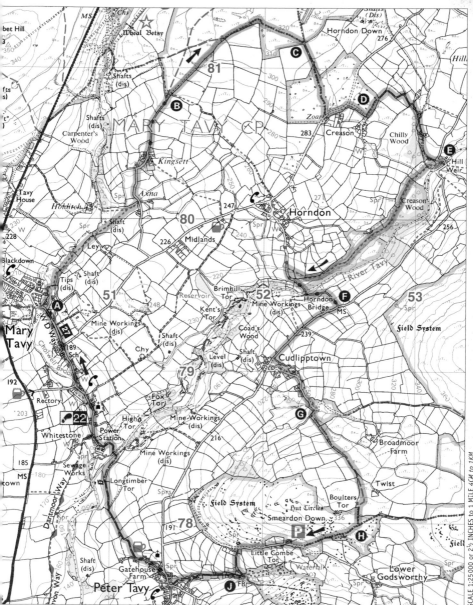

length of made-up lane. This bears sharply to the left (and becomes unkempt) at a signpost saying 'Public Bridlepath Hill Bridge', waymarked in blue **D**. This is pleasant walking, with Hare Tor a prominent feature ahead. The bridleway leads via several gates through Hillbridge Farm and Chilly Wood and past Old School House, to a lane; turn right towards the bridge, where the rushing waters of the Tavy look inviting on a hot day. Before reaching the bridge turn right **E** down wooden steps to access the riverbank. Cross the leat and turn right along a narrow concrete way, then follow the left bank of the leat through Creason Wood. This leat is a remarkable work, running 100ft (30m) or so above the river to reach a reservoir 1 mile (1.6km) distant.

Some of its channel has been chiselled through granite. The footpath does not seem to be over-popular.

At last this idyllic section comes to an end when the path meets a track. Turn left downhill and follow it to Horndon Bridge, and then steeply up the other side to meet a lane. Turn right **F** at the top of the lane to Cudlipptown, noticing the fine old milestone and the views west to Brent Tor. At Cudlipptown bear to the left as the post-box comes into view along the path that runs on top of a bank. This leads to the made-up lane passing the farm; bear left uphill. When this emerges into open countryside with a rushing stream running close by, turn right **G** over a clapper bridge. Bear left uphill, with a wall right (the blue-waymarked signpost is well concealed and reads 'Public Bridle-path to the Moor'). Pass through a gate and continue uphill with the wall right – a fairly strenuous climb – to pass through a small gate in the wall ahead. Keep the intake wall on the right to skirt Boulters Tor via a gate. Look back and you will appreciate how far you have travelled: Wheal Betsy is tiny, just below the skyline. Pass through a gate marked by a signpost pointing in the reverse direction. Descend to meet a track and turn right **H**.

Continue downhill, turning right at the lane. Just before the farm on the left, look left for a gate – the middle of three – signed to 'The Combe'. This descends to an enchanting dell with a stream and foot-bridge. Do not cross the stream, but turn right **J** along the bank. This bridleway becomes a lane lined with cottages. Just beyond the bridge turn right along a short section of bridleway to the centre of Peter Tavy. Turn right to reach the church (as beautiful inside as outside). Bear left past the lychgate, then right to pass the pub. The next bridleway right leads back to Mary Tavy, crossing the River Tavy en route, a delightful end to a walk brimming with beauty and interest. ●

The beautiful church at Mary Tavy

New Bridge and Dr Blackall's Drive

		GPS waypoints	
Start	New Bridge	🗺	SX 711 708
Distance	6 miles (9.7km)	**A**	SX 714 715
Approximate time	3 hours	**B**	SX 716 720
Parking	New Bridge	**C**	SX 711 729
Refreshments	Pub and café at Holne (off route)	**D**	SX 700 736
Ordnance Survey maps	Landrangers 191 (Okehampton & North Dartmoor) and 202 (Torbay & South Dartmoor), Explorer OL28 (Dartmoor)	**E**	SX 700 730
		F	SX 695 731
		G	SX 704 713

This walk enjoys a tremendous range of beautiful scenery, including a lovely wooded section along the Dart river as well as superb panoramic views over the Dart gorge and Webburn valley. The first half of the walk is a long uphill push through woods and fields, but the superlative views along Dr Blackall's Drive compensate for the effort expended. Care should be taken when the route briefly follows the Ashburton–Princetown road, which is busy at weekends and during holiday periods.

The granite 'new bridge' over the River Dart, originally a packhorse bridge, was new in the 15th century. It spans a particularly attractive stretch of the river, which flows through a thickly wooded and steep-sided gorge both upstream and downstream and it makes an excellent starting point both for gentle riverside and woodland rambles and for more strenuous and challenging moorland hikes.

🗺 Walk down steps on the riverbank side of the car park, pass under the bridge and along a most delightful riverside path, through woods and across meadows, to a lane **A**. Turn right along the lane for ¼ mile (400m) and then turn left up a narrower lane signposted to Lower Town. Where the lane bears sharp right keep ahead on an uphill footpath **B** through a gate into woodland. Pass over a stile at the top and along the right edge of a field, then through the left of two gates. Keep along the right edge of fields, and through a gate onto a lane. Turn right; as the lane bears sharp left turn right as signed through a gate. Keep along the left edge of fields, eventually passing through a gate onto a track by houses. Keep ahead to a lane and turn left steeply uphill **C**.

Past Leusdon church the lane levels off and, at the first junction, keep ahead past Leusdon Common on the left, bearing right at the next junction along a wider road, signed Ponsworthy. Where this road bends left just past the sign for Ponsworthy, turn left **D** at the drive to Sweaton Farm. Bear left through a gate, and pass to the left of the farm. Walk gently uphill; turn right at an open gateway, and immediately left through a gate into an enclosed path.

The picturesque River Dart above New Bridge

Follow this to a gate. Go through, keep ahead along the edge of a field by a hedge on the left, turn left over a stile and continue along the edge of the next field, this time with the hedge on the right, to another stile. Climb over, turn left along a lane and, in a few yards, turn sharp right **E** along the Princetown road, following it uphill towards the open moor to reach the parking area at Bel Tor Corner on the left.

From here the all-round views are magnificent: to the west the TV transmitter on North Hessary Tor and, below it, the grim buildings of the convict prison, to the east Haytor, to the south the Dart Gorge and Venford reservoir, and to the north across the Webburn valley towards Widecombe in the Moor. At the car park turn left **F** and, keeping by a wall on the left, head towards Mel Tor in front, between Bel Tor on the left and Sharp Tor on the right, soon turning left along a broad, walled track. This is Dr Blackall's Drive, laid out by the gentleman of that name in the 19th century so that

he could enjoy the glorious views while riding in his carriage. Within a few yards you will realise just how stunning these views are, for you follow the drive for the next 1½ miles (2.4km) across open grassland studded with gorse, fern and heather along the top edge of the Dart Gorge. This must rank as one of the finest stretches of walking on Dartmoor, with glorious scenery allied with a good, firm, wide, well-drained track.

The drive drops down below the slopes of Aish Tor on the left. At a path junction just past a disused, fenced-off quarry on the right, turn right **G** on the left of two grassy tracks leading to a quarry road. Cross over, continue down to a narrow lane, cross that and keep ahead downhill – through bracken and gorse – with a wall below right. Meet the road on a sharp bend and follow it downhill to New Bridge. ●

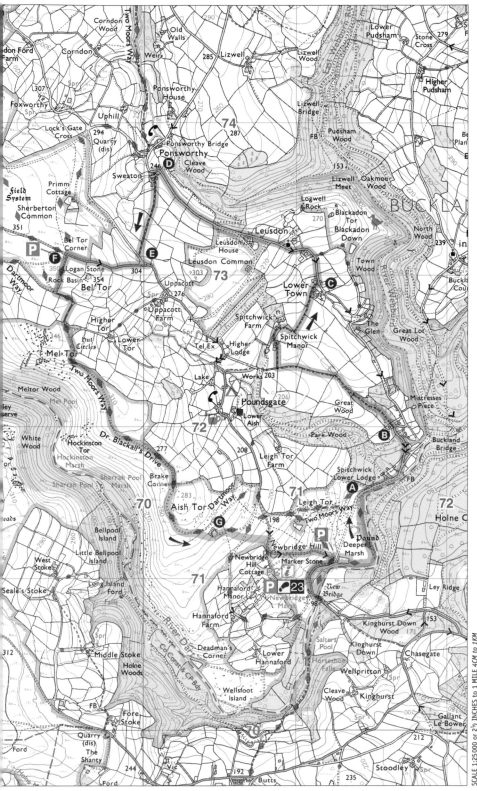

SCALE 1:25000 or 2½ INCHES to 1 MILE 4CM to 1KM

Princetown, Whiteworks and Crock of Gold

Start	Princetown
Distance	7½ miles (12.1km)
Approximate time	3½ hours
Parking	Princetown
Refreshments	Pubs and cafés in Princetown
Ordnance Survey maps	Landrangers 191 (Okehampton & North Dartmoor) and 202 (Torbay & South Dartmoor), Explorer OL28 (Dartmoor)

GPS waypoints

- 🖉 SX 590 734
- Ⓐ SX 597 723
- Ⓑ SX 603 704
- Ⓒ SX 612 710
- Ⓓ SX 615 714
- Ⓔ SX 624 727
- Ⓕ SX 603 733

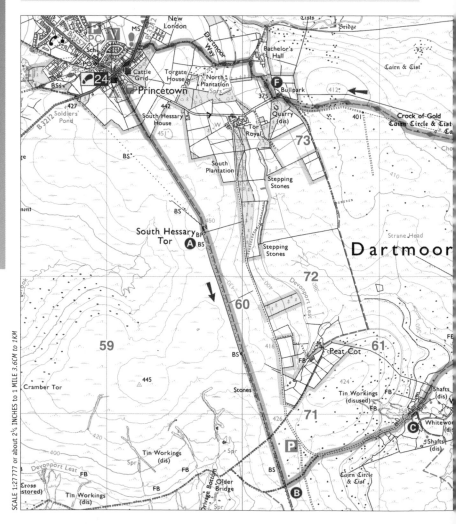

SCALE 1:27 777 or about 2¼ INCHES to 1 MILE 3.6CM to 1KM

This is almost entirely a walk on the open moor and, as such, can provide an excellent opportunity to sample the unique flavour of Dartmoor, inhospitable as this can be. The two stream crossings after Whiteworks are typical hazards, but the great beauty of the wilderness that follows is more than adequate compensation. More than anything, the walk shows the wisdom of locating the prison here – this countryside offers few places of refuge for the convict on the run.

'Grim' and 'bleak' are adjectives often used to describe both Princetown and its surroundings and, on a grey and misty day, neither can be described as inviting. Furthermore the town possesses Dartmoor's least attractive, if most famous (or, to be more accurate, infamous) building – the

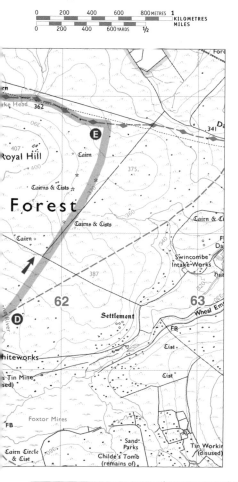

prison, which appears to match its setting perfectly. Princetown was founded by Thomas Tyrwhitt in the late 18th century. He was Lord Warden of the Stannaries, Secretary of the Duchy of Cornwall and a friend of the then Prince of Wales. Tyrwhitt hoped to develop the area into a flourishing agricultural community and attract people here. His agricultural dream failed but it was Tyrwhitt who founded the prison here. It originally housed French prisoners from the Napoleonic Wars but later prisoners from the war with America were also held at Princetown. Today the prison is still in use, housing up to 600 prisoners.

The walk begins from the town centre, between the two pubs – the Plume of Feathers and the Railway Inn – from where a track leads onto the moor. It climbs gently uphill, with a wall on the left at the start, to the summit of South Hessary Tor **A**. Some way beyond, by a boundary stone, the wall bends to the left away from the track (this is not shown on the map). Note that the boundary stones marked by the Ordnance Survey are not the prominent stones put up by the PCWW (Plymouth Corporation Water Works) in 1917: these are numerous and are not represented (they delineate the catchment area of the Plymouth waterworks). Many of the boundary stones marked on the map have been toppled over. A well-used track crosses the path; this comes from Burrator and goes to Peat Cot. Keep straight ahead past an ancient boundary stone and a PCWW marker, side by side. Drop down 100 yds (92m) to another path crossing **B**; turn left. Cross a further track and keep straight ahead over rough grassland to reach a tarmac lane. Turn right. The lane ends at the old tin-mining settlement of Whiteworks **C**.

Carry straight on through the old mine-workings (whose heyday was around 1820). Go through a field gate onto open moorland; follow the grassy bridlepath straight ahead. The path drops down to a stream; the crossing point is not obvious, but the stream is narrow enough just below a large granite boulder **D**. *Note that from this point the obvious route on the ground runs roughly parallel to but north of the bridlepath marked on the map.* Follow the grassy path uphill across remote moorland; notorious Foxtor Mire lies only ½ mile (800m) to the south. This 'quaker' once claimed the life of an escaped Dartmoor prisoner and was the inspiration for the 'Great Grimpen Mire' of Conan Doyle's *The Hound of the Baskervilles*.

Over the hill the beaten path is still clear, running in a north-easterly direction. Look right for views of the Swincombe valley; note that the boundary crossing the path on the map no longer exists, apart from the odd fencepost. Cross a ditch and later, as the next hill is crested at a solitary post, wonderful views of

Bellever Tor, flanked by dark conifers, lie ahead. Drop gently downhill over rough grassland to meet a grassy track at right angles with a fence ahead **E**. Turn left along the line of one of Dartmoor's oldest tracks and climb gently uphill, heading straight for the TV mast in the distance. The path later gives way to a better-surfaced gritty track, the result of the hard labour of conscientious objectors during the First World War; the war ended before the track could be completed. The granite buildings of the Dartmoor Training Centre can be seen right, with the pyramidal shape of Liddaford Tor beyond. The Crock of Gold turns out to be an untidy cairn amongst scattered rocks, though the cist itself lies about 30 yds (27m) from the track. A stream is crossed, then a long, straight, uphill section of track ends with a descent to a gate at Bullpark **F**. Pass through; turn right after the house on a bridleway. Pass through another gate and continue up the track. Turn left at a bridlepath junction, with Bachelor's Hall below right. Go through a gate over the Devonport Leat, and follow the track uphill before descending towards Princetown. Note the remains of the old crossing-gate of the Princetown railway just before the track meets the main road. Turn left for the town centre. ●

A view of Princetown, high on western Dartmoor

Two Bridges, Wistman's Wood and the West Dart

		GPS waypoints
Start	Two Bridges	🖉 SX 609 750
Distance	9 miles (14.5km)	**Ⓐ** SX 610 756
Approximate time	6 hours	**Ⓑ** SX 612 767
Parking	Opposite Two Bridges Hotel	**Ⓒ** SX 612 775
Refreshments	Two Bridges Hotel	**Ⓓ** SX 616 778
Ordnance Survey maps	Landranger 191 (Okehampton & North Dartmoor), Explorer OL28 (Dartmoor)	**Ⓔ** SX 618 775
		Ⓕ SX 627 773
		Ⓖ SX 637 776
		Ⓗ SX 644 772
		Ⓙ SX 645 746
		Ⓚ SX 648 737
		Ⓛ SX 642 733
		Ⓜ SX 635 730
		Ⓝ SX 625 742

This is an ideal walk, with lots of wonderful scenery. Crossing the stepping stones over the West Dart can be a problem and, if the river is running high, it is advisable not to attempt it.

The walk begins from the car park opposite the Two Bridges Hotel.

🖉 Go through the gate signed 'Wistman's Wood' and follow the broad, sandy track with the summit of Longaford Tor ahead. After ½ mile (800m) the path passes Crockern **Ⓐ**, swinging to the right past a cottage. To the right is Crockern Tor, famous as the ancient meeting place of the Stannary Parliament, which dealt with the laws relating to tin-mining. This location was chosen for its central position on Dartmoor. Keep roughly parallel to the valley of the West Dart on the left; the stubby oak trees of Wistman's Wood, one of only three patches of ancient oak woodland remaining on the moor, appear ahead. Cross a stile by a noticeboard **Ⓑ**, giving information on the wood's ecological importance and the efforts being made to preserve it. Keep the wood on the left and, about 500 yds (457m) before the last clump of trees, strike up the slope on the right **Ⓒ**, soon finding a rough path that leads to the saddle between the two outcrops of Longaford Tor **Ⓓ**. It is an easy climb, and

the summit a superb viewpoint.

Walk south (right) from the tor, keeping roughly parallel to a wall below left. Bear left towards a gateway in that wall; pass through this **Ⓔ** onto rough grassland. The clear path ahead leads to boggy ground, so bear right and then left on higher ground towards the northern-most chimney of Powdermills. The ancient Lichway runs across this area.

Pass through a gate **Ⓕ** opposite the chimney, and follow the signed path towards the Cherry Brook. The old buildings hereabouts were part of a gunpowder factory, and placed well apart to reduce

Trekkers pause on the flank of Bellever Tor

the risk of a catastrophe. Bear left to cross the Cherry Brook as signed. Follow the Lichway, bearing right uphill and through a gate onto moorland. Bear left on the bridlepath to reach the road, site of a famous Dartmoor tradition: this is where the Hairy Hands grab the steering wheel from the grasp of a driver, often fatally.

Cross the road **G** into Forestry Commission land. The Lichway dates from medieval times: villagers from Bellever took corpses to Lydford for Christian burial – 11 miles (17.5km). After some distance along a forest track, crossing another en route, turn left at a T-junction. Cross over the next track, and continue to reach the edge of a wide fire break **H**. Turn right towards Bellever Tor, bearing left along a wall, then right again to climb up to the tor – well worth it for the view.

Keep ahead across the tor and descend in a southerly direction, heading for the large newtake with Laughter Tor on its eastern edge (left). Pass through a five-bar gate in the wall at the bottom of the slope, then keep the wall on the right and follow it, eventually passing through another gate at Dunnabridge **J**.

Turn left at the road and, after 200 yds (184m), follow a path on the right that leaves the road obliquely to reach the blue-waymarked bridleway leading down to the West Dart River. The path follows the sparkling river to the stepping stones **K**, which provide the only way across. The path now follows the River Swincombe, which joins the Dart at the stepping stones. This river is also crossed by stepping stones, but the river is narrower.

At the lane turn sharply to the right to reach Sherberton and pass through the farmyard following blue waymarks, bearing left along a walled track that ultimately leads to Little Sherberton. Pass through the gate at the end of the track and bear half-left across the field, following a bridlepath sign **L**. Keep parallel to the wall on the left and drop to the right of a

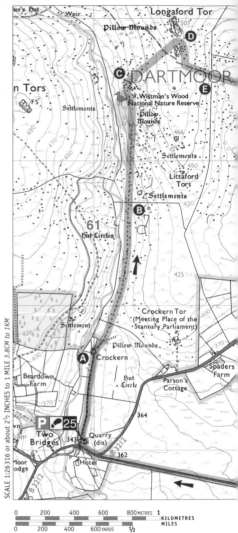

SCALE 1:26316 or about 2½ INCHES to 1 MILE 3.8CM to 1KM

stone circle. Make for a signpost in the wall at the top of the hill ahead. Pass through the gate; keep straight ahead on a grassy path (seemingly into the middle of nowhere) to find another signpost **M**.

Turn right along a clear path. Follow this downhill through a gate and over a ford, then through another gate and down to cross the bridge, with the Dartmoor Training Centre right. Follow the drive uphill, eventually reaching the beech-lined drive to the Prince Hall Hotel. Turn right **N** to meet the road; turn left and follow the road (take care) back to Two Bridges. ●

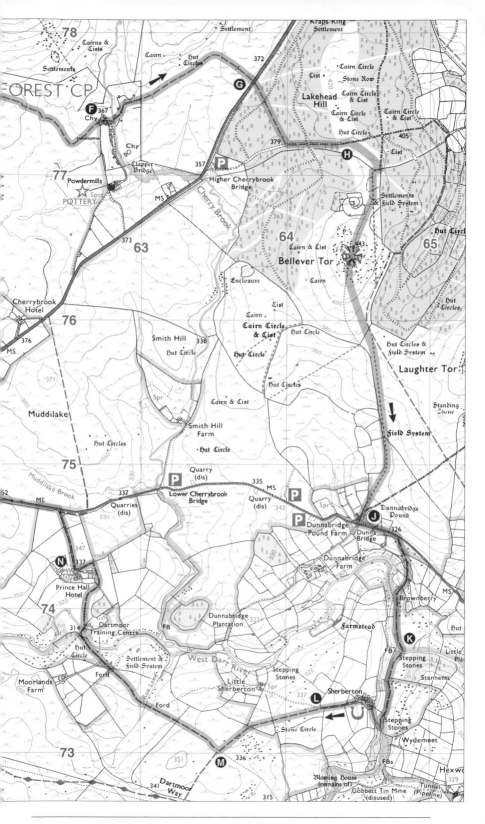

Grimspound, Coombe Down and Challacombe

		GPS waypoints	
Start	Bennett's Cross, about two miles (3km) north-east of Postbridge on the B3212	✏	SX 679 815
		Ⓐ	SX 691 817
Distance	9½ miles (15.3km) or two separate walks of 4½ miles (7.2km) each	Ⓑ	SX 692 816
		Ⓒ	SX 696 809
		Ⓓ	SX 706 809
Approximate time	5½ hours (3 hours and 2½ hours for the two separate walks)	Ⓔ	SX 720 802
		Ⓕ	SX 714 824
		Ⓖ	SX 709 825
Parking	At Bennett's Cross or nearby	Ⓗ	SX 699 816
Refreshments	Warren House Inn	Ⓙ	SX 693 810
Ordnance Survey maps	Landranger 191 (Okehampton & North Dartmoor), Explorer OL28 (Dartmoor)	Ⓚ	SX 692 793
		Ⓛ	SX 681 810

This is another of those Dartmoor walks which seems to have just enough of everything. Getting bored of the open moor? Then take to the woods. Had enough of the woods? Then how about a field or two? This is a figure of eight route which, if necessary, can be divided into two shorter walks, both of which are interesting. There is a lay-by below Hookney Tor Ⓒ, where the path to Grimspound begins, which might be considered as an alternative starting point.

✏ From Bennett's Cross take the Two Moors Way, which leads away left through the heather, with Birch Tor away to the right. You should soon pass a stone shelter on the right. Over the crest of the hill Shapley Tor comes into view ahead and you should see an old boundary stone amidst the heather on the right. Where the path splits Ⓐ, keep straight ahead, dropping downhill towards the road Ⓑ. Turn right for about ½ mile (800m) until you come to a small lay-by on the right and a well-trodden path on the left Ⓒ, which ascends to Grimspound, bearing right to a stream en route.

Grimspound is the most impressive of Dartmoor's ancient settlements. The perimeter wall, which was once at least 102ft (31m) high, enclosed an area of 4 acres (1.6 ha) containing 24 small round houses. The remains of these structures on this bleak hillside give us a stark reminder of the rigours of prehistoric life on Dartmoor, when dense forest covered the floors of the valleys, leaving the tops of the moors as highways.

Cross the settlement to the exit on the far side (opposite where you entered). The path is pretty level, and heads east, initially passing between Hookney and Hameldon Tors. Where the path forks Ⓓ, ignore the right branch and keep straight on. The path starts to descend; 20 yds (20m) to the right you will see an RAF memorial stone. A wood comes into view below left and you should keep this on the left and continue downhill, aiming for the far corner. Just before the road is reached at Natsworthy, there is a stile **ⓔ** on the left into a wood. Climb this and follow the clear yellow-waymarked path through the trees, bearing right at a T-junction. Emerge from the woods just before Heathercombe and climb a stile to make for a gate to the right of a house. Cross a metalled road to find a footpath by a cottage (Heathercombe North) signposted to Moor Gate. Continue following yellow waymarks through the woods until these end with a stile and a stream. Cross both and make for a field-gate across a meadow. Pass through this and through another field to reach the stile that crosses the farm track near Kendon Farm. Cross a stile then strike across another field to a

Grimspound – the most impressive of Dartmoor's ancient settlements

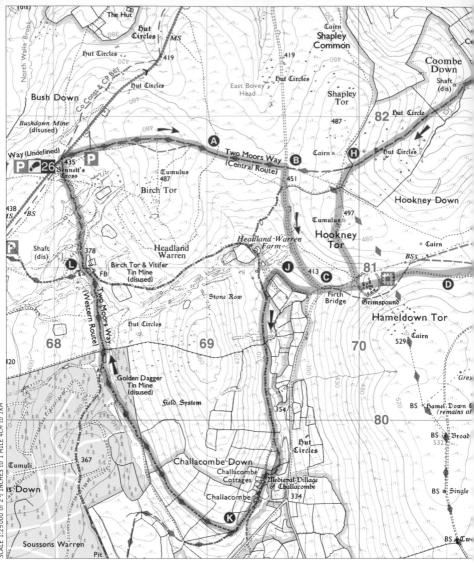

SCALE 1:25000 or 2½ INCHES to 1 MILE 4CM to 1KM

0	200	400	600	800 METRES	1
0	200	400	600 YARDS	½	KILOMETRES MILES

signed stile in the fence in the far right corner. Follow signs to cross the small stream in the middle of the next field; bear right, keeping the hedge left. Cross the next stile, then another into a green lane on your left. Just before the farmyard, turn left up a bank and over a stile into a field. Bear right uphill, to cross a stile and keep ahead behind Lower Hookner farmhouse until you reach the farm track via a gate **F**.

Bear left up the track. Pass through a gate on the right almost immediately; turn left and keep close to the hedge, to a gate. Cross the next field to pass through a yellow-waymarked gate over a stream. Keep ahead up the field and go through another gate. Cross the next field to a stile on the edge of trees and reach West Coombe. The stream here has to be crossed with a jump. Walk straight ahead to meet a track, and turn left in the yard **G**.

Now follow the concrete track that goes to the old mine manager's house, keeping the derelict mine workings on your left.

summit. Descend to Grimspound, then turn right downhill to reach the lay-by by the start of the Grimspound walk **G**.

Cross the road and continue downhill on a narrow path through bracken to reach the track leading to Headland Warren Farm. Turn right towards the farmhouse. About 100 yds (92m) before reaching it, immediately after passing through a gateway, turn left **J** down to a gate, marked bridlepath for Challacombe Farm. This gives onto a pleasant, level track which runs due south parallel to the road above. The broken ground is due to old mine-workings, a characteristic feature of this leg of the walk. Stay on the blue-waymarked track, eventually going through a gate to pass Challacombe Cottages, and through another onto a concrete drive.

Keep ahead to pass to the left of Challacombe Farm, then follow the track uphill, and soon a choice of footpaths is offered **K**. Here bear right to Bennett's Cross. A forest soon appears on the left, and the track descends to run through a gate and along its edge, passing varied mining remains. As the path progresses there is a good view of craggy Birch Tor on the right.

Where the track bears sharp left, keep ahead, by a drainage channel, and pass through a gate. There follows a delightful stretch along the floor of the valley, passing through more old mine workings, some of them potentially dangerous. Where the clapper bridge crosses the stream, a path on the left leads to the Warren House Inn, which is about ten minutes away.

To return to Bennett's Cross, keep ahead with the stream left. Where the path bears sharp left, take the narrow path right uphill **L** which winds through the old workings. Climb out of the end of a deep gully and bear left to reach the path; turn right towards the cross on the skyline ahead, situated near the parking area. ●

Leave this driveway when it makes a hairpin to the right to reach the house. The track continues to follow the course of the stream uphill, eventually abandoning the latter to climb to the moor and passing a pond on the left. The pleasant grassy track soon passes by old hut circles. Look for a gate in the wall on the skyline **H**. Make for this and, after passing through it, turn left; keep the wall left and climb towards Hookney Tor. At the top of the wall make for the Tor by passing through a 'gateway' of two perpendicular stones. A well-marked path leads to the

Holne Moor and Snowdon

		GPS waypoints
Start	Holne	
Distance	9 miles (14.5km)	✐ SX 706 694
Parking	Holne village car park or along the lanes round the village centre	Ⓐ SX 706 691 Ⓑ SX 704 685 Ⓒ SX 684 680 Ⓓ SX 683 674
Approximate time	4½ hours	Ⓔ SX 672 673
Refreshments	Pubs at Holne and Scorriton, café at Holne	Ⓕ SX 659 690 Ⓖ SX 672 697
Ordnance Survey maps	Landranger 202 (Torbay & South Dartmoor), Explorer OL28 (Dartmoor)	Ⓗ SX 679 696 Ⓙ SX 686 701 Ⓚ SX 693 700 Ⓛ SX 694 697 Ⓜ SX 693 695 Ⓝ SX 695 689

Even on days with good visibility a compass is essential on this walk *which takes you over moorland to a remote and lonely ridge. The way down from Ryder's Hill is over rough ground and finding the correct line of descent can be difficult with no obvious path to follow, though if you keep heading eastwards you can hardly fail to meet the Hexworthy road. The lower sections of the walk are on country lanes and bridleways festooned with wild flowers in spring and early summer.*

✐ Turn left out of the car park at Holne and left again towards Scorriton at the top of the hill. About 150 yds (137m) after this junction, when the lane swings right Ⓐ, keep ahead on a track that is obviously unsuitable for motor vehicles. The rocky bridleway descends steeply to meet a lane. Bear right to cross the stream and then right again off the main road to climb a lane into Scorriton. Turn right at a T-junction and then immediately left Ⓑ onto a dead end lane signposted to the moor via Chalk Ford.

The track climbs gently up to the moor. Pause occasionally to enjoy the views back. Where the track bears right through a gate keep ahead, eventually passing through another gate on the bridlepath to Chalk Ford – there is a deer enclosure on the right. The little River Mardle is crossed

by a footbridge at Chalk Ford Ⓒ – an ideal spot for a picnic. Turn left after the bridge to follow the fence uphill and cross another small stream. There are woods to the left at this point but later the path runs to the right of a wall. Ford the little stream at the wall corner Ⓓ before reaching Lud Gate, and bear half-right towards beech trees standing by another wall. Before reaching this turn right on one of several tracks which climb Pupers Hill, heading west. The rocky cairn on Pupers Rock Ⓔ is soon reached, with a fantastic view over desolate Huntingdon Warren.

From the tor head north westwards (right) on the faint path along the ridge to Snowdon which bears no resemblance to its namesake. Its ramparts are the spoil heaps of tin workings and there are two rough cairns. On a clear day you can see

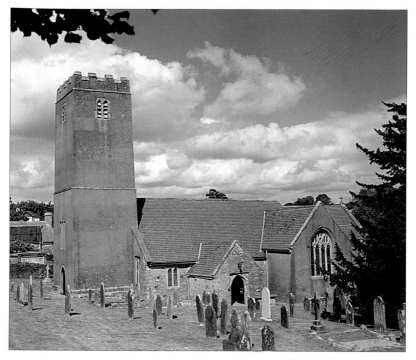

The church at Holne

the Teign estuary and Lyme Bay. Keep on walking in a northwesterly direction towards the TV mast on North Hessary Tor to reach the next summit, Ryder's Hill, which has boundary stones and a triangulation pillar **F**.

Turn sharply right from here to walk east–north-easterly across open ground with the unmistakable shape of Haytor in the distance ahead. There is also the occasional boundary stone to follow. You will pass the head of the River Mardle and more old mine workings. The sweeping panorama and the song of skylarks make this an enjoyable – if vague – part of the route as you steadily descend towards two boundary stones close together. These mark the line of the Sandy Way **G** – an escape route off the moor in bad weather. Follow this grassy path downhill, soon passing a lone hawthorn tree. Just after passing two more boundary stones bear left **H** on a descending grassy path, with views over Venford reservoir to the left.

The path joins a track **J**; turn right, heading for a group of conifers in the distance.

The track crosses a dry leat on stone slabs; at the next stream (flowing south-eastwards) turn right **K** and walk along the bank. Note the sign stating that this leat is an essential animal water supply. Follow the leat to where it meets another leat **L**, and there is another sign.

Bear left for a few yards, then turn right to cross the leat. Follow a faint path which heads southwest, descending and heading almost straight towards Pupers Hill on the horizon. The path drops steeply through stands of gorse, with the steep-sided valley of Great Combe below right, to reach a small gate leading off the moor **M**.

Follow the path steeply downhill, with glorious views to the west. Pass through another gate, and descend to meet a track by a path sign. Turn right and follow the shady track downhill. Cross a ford at

Greatcombe, pass through a gate and follow a rough track to meet the start of a tarmac lane where the Sandy Way descends from the moor on the right 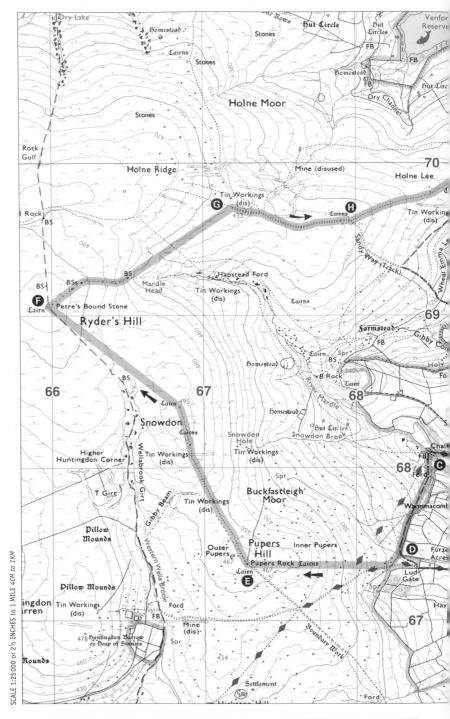.

Turn left onto the road which leads into Michelcombe. Keep ahead and cross a bridge when the road to Scorriton goes to the right. Where the lane meets the Holne-to-Hexworthy road, go straight across to climb steps to a footpath, which leads into Holne churchyard. Emerge onto the road by the Church House Inn and turn right for the car park and village café.

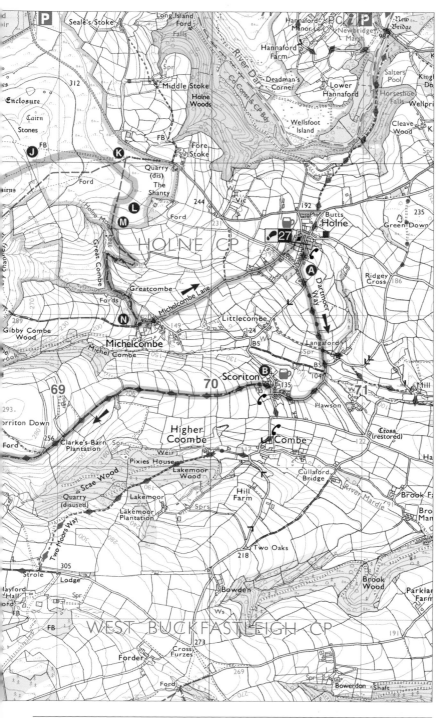

Ringmoor Down, Eylesbarrow and Siward's Cross

		GPS waypoints
Start	Near Ringmoor Cottage, due south of Sheepstor village	✐ SX 559 669
Distance	9 miles (14.5km)	Ⓐ SX 579 673
Approximate time	5 hours	Ⓑ SX 598 681
		Ⓒ SX 604 699
Parking	Off the road near Ringmoor Cottage	Ⓓ SX 611 695
		Ⓔ SX 613 692
Refreshments	None	Ⓕ SX 610 684
Ordnance Survey maps	Landranger 202 (Torbay & South Dartmoor), Explorer OL28 (Dartmoor)	Ⓖ SX 607 682
		Ⓗ SX 603 675
		Ⓙ SX 592 670
		Ⓚ SX 583 662
		Ⓛ SX 576 664

This is a harder walk than it might look at first glance as it needs some skill (or luck) in navigation. However, common sense and good map-reading should ensure an enjoyable walk through truly rugged country. A compass is also advisable. Some of the names of the valleys – Drizzle Combe, Evil Combe – are uninviting and hardly do justice to the great beauty of the scenery. The archaeological treasures of Drizzle Combe are impressive even for Dartmoor.

✐ Leave the car on the green sward just above Ringmoor Cottage, on the left of the lane overlooking Burrator reservoir and set off up the lane with Sheepstor ahead. At a junction bear right, signed Nattor, and when you come to the stream Ⓐ that marks the end of the made-up lane, cross it and begin the climb to Eylesbarrow.

Pass the old scout hut – now Guttor Tor Refuge, used for adventure training – in trees on the right. The ascent is long but not steep. The stones marked PCWW mark the extent of the Plymouth Waterworks catchment area and the views to the left over Burrator reservoir are outstanding. The track levels, then climbs again; note the remains of an old mining building on

the right. Keep on the main track which soon reaches the scanty remains of Eylesbarrow Tin Mine Ⓑ. This was worked between 1815–1852 and once employed 60 men.

A path branches off to the right here but keep on the main track, which climbs left through the site, then levels off before descending towards Nun's Cross. Nun's Cross Farm comes into view on the right and, in a little while, Nun's Cross itself is seen ahead. Otherwise known as Siward's Cross Ⓒ, it was probably a 13th-century boundary mark of the Forest of Dartmoor.

From the cross turn right over an old wall to pass behind the farm (now used for adventure training). Keep ahead on an indistinct path, skirting tufts of sedge on the right, before bearing right towards a clear path to a bridge over the Devonport Leat and the ford of a small stream. Note a prominent boulder on the hillside almost straight ahead, the only landmark in an otherwise featureless landscape: that is your next port of call. Follow the grassy track uphill from the ford, keeping right at a vague fork **D**. Keep uphill, passing to

the right of an old cross, which stands upright on the banks of a reave (an ancient boundary ditch, usually medieval though some are prehistoric).

When you reach the boulder **E**, look right uphill to find another triangular-shaped one close by, surmounted by a small brass cross. Keep ahead, bearing left across open moorland – a compass bearing is useful here – in a south–south-

One of the prehistoric monoliths in remote Drizzle Combe

westerly direction. If you look back Nun's Cross Farm will soon pass out of sight, but the TV mast on South Hessary tor should soon be behind your right shoulder. Ahead Gnats' Head, with its distinctive cairn, is prominent to the southeast, while soon the system of tracks converging on Plym Ford will be seen below. There is a dark mini-ravine on the left.

Thread your way towards the ford through the old tin workings, meeting the track which, to the right, returns to Eylesbarrow. Follow the track to the ford **F**. Do not cross the Plym; keep it on the left and head downstream on a narrow path. Rejoin the Eylesbarrow track; on a left bend cross a small stream, then bear left off the track **G** to follow a disused leat. Follow the leat as it runs along the contours. Avoid the bog of Evil Combe by crossing it high up, and keep heading for the left side of Lower Hartor Tor.

From the tor **H** drop downhill and follow the river to pass Plym Steps, where the Langcombe Brook joins the Plym, (the latter is the smaller stream). There follows a pleasant walk along the bank of the infant river, though the easier walking is on the valley side a little way above. The sea glints in the sunshine in the far distance.

The valley broadens dramatically; this is Drizzle Combe, one of the most important of Dartmoor's prehistoric sites and a place that can have altered little since it was abandoned by the people of the Bronze Age. Three menhirs dominate the basin, each with a fine stone row, along with countless hut circles, all the more impressive for being found in such a remote and evocative location.

Bear right away from the river to find the tallest menhir on Dartmoor **J**. Head downhill to pass the next, then bear left towards the river to find a ford across a tributary stream. (This area can get very boggy; in times of wet weather skirt right around the edge of the basin.) Head uphill, aiming for the trees ahead that mark Ditsworthy Warren House **K**, another ancient building which now serves as an adventure centre. Behind the house is a yard walled in by huge boulders, offset to provide an overhang to prevent the warrener's dogs from escaping. From here

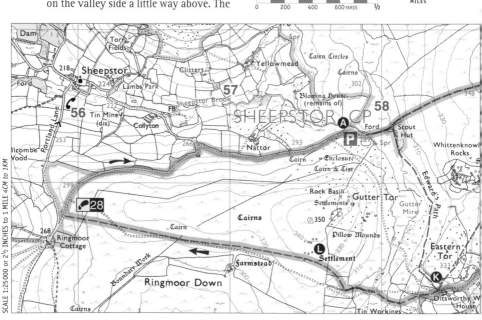

the shorter route strikes north (right) along the track below Gutter Tor. To return to Ringmoor Cottage, take the lower track leading directly from the house to the west. Follow it downhill over a stream; bear right uphill at a fork of tracks, bearing right again at the top to reach a gate on the skyline **L**, where a sign points to Ringmoor Cottage. The route across this stretch of bare moorland is marked by posts. When trees appear on the skyline make to the right of them to find a field-gate and the starting point near Ringmoor Cottage.

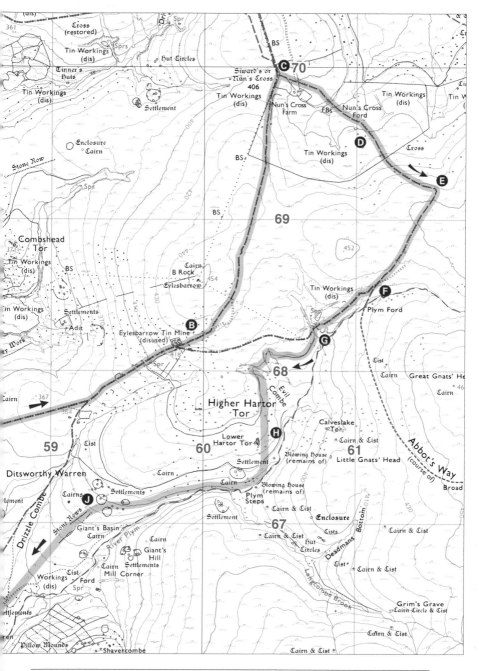

Further Information

The National Parks and Countryside Recreation

Ten national parks were created in England and Wales as a result of an Act of Parliament in 1949. In addition to these, there are numerous specially designated Areas of Outstanding Natural Beauty, Country and Regional Parks, Sites of Special Scientific Interest and picnic areas scattered throughout England, Wales and Scotland, all of which share the twin aims of preservation of the countryside and public accessibility and enjoyment.

The National Parks and Countryside Act of 1949 provided for the designation and preservation of areas both of great scenic beauty and of particular wildlife and scientific interest throughout Britain. More specifically it provided for the creation of national parks in England and Wales. Scotland was excluded because, with greater areas of open space and a smaller population, there were fewer pressures on the Scottish countryside.

A National Parks Commission, a forerunner of the Countryside Commission, was set up, and over the next eight years ten areas were designated as parks; seven in England (Northumberland, Lake District, North York Moors, Yorkshire Dales, Peak District, Exmoor and Dartmoor) and three in Wales (Snowdonia, Brecon Beacons and Pembrokeshire Coast). In 1989 the Norfolk and Suffolk Broads were added to the list. At the same time the Commission was also given the responsibility for designating other smaller areas of high recreational and scenic qualities (Areas of Outstanding Natural Beauty), plus the power to propose and develop long-distance footpaths, now called National Trails.

The authorities who administer the individual national parks have the very difficult task of reconciling the interests of the people who live and earn their living within them with those of visitors.

In the end it all comes down to a question of balance between conservation and 'sensitive development'. On the one hand there is a responsibility to preserve the natural beauty of the national parks and to promote their enjoyment by the public, and on the other, the needs and well-being of the people living and working in them have to be borne in mind.

The National Trust

Anyone who likes visiting places of natural beauty and/or historic interest has cause to be grateful to the National Trust. Without it, many such places would probably have vanished.

The purpose of the National Trust is to preserve areas of natural beauty and sites of historic interest by acquisition, holding them in trust for the nation and making them available for public access and enjoyment. Some of its properties have been acquired through purchase, but many of the Trust's properties have been donated. Nowadays it is not only one of the biggest landowners in the country, but also one of the most active conservation charities, protecting 581,113 acres (253,176 ha) of land, including 555 miles (892km) of coastline, and over 300 historic properties in England, Wales and Northern Ireland. (There is a separate National Trust for Scotland, which was set up in 1931.

As it works towards its dual aims of conserving areas of attractive countryside and encouraging greater public access (not easy to reconcile in this age of mass tourism), the Trust provides an excellent service for walkers by creating new concessionary paths and waymarked trails, maintaining stiles and foot bridges and combating the ever-increasing problem of footpath erosion.

For details of membership, contact the National Trust at the addresses on page 95.

The Ramblers' Association

No organisation works more actively to protect and extend the rights and interests of walkers in the countryside than the Ramblers' Association. Its aims are clear: to foster a greater knowledge, love and care of the countryside; to assist in the protection and enhancement of public rights of way and areas of natural beauty; to work for greater public access to the countryside; and to encourage more people to take up rambling as a healthy, recreational leisure activity.

It was founded in 1935 when, following the setting up of a National Council of Ramblers' Federation in 1931, a number of federations in London, Manchester, the Midlands and elsewhere came together to create a more effective pressure group, to deal with such problems as the disappearance or obstruction of footpaths, the prevention of access to open mountain and moorland, and increasing hostility from landowners. This was the era of the mass trespasses, when there were sometimes violent confrontations between ramblers and gamekeepers, especially on the moorlands of the Peak District.

Since then the Ramblers' Association has played a key role in preserving and developing the national footpath network, supporting the creation of national parks and encouraging the designation and waymarking of long-distance routes.

Our freedom of access to the countryside, now enshrined in legislation, is still in its early years and requires constant vigilance. But over and above this there will always be the problem of footpaths being illegally obstructed, disappearing through lack of use, or being extinguished by housing or road construction.

It is to meet such problems and dangers that the Ramblers' Association exists and represents the interests of all walkers. The address to write to for information on the Ramblers' Association and how to become a member is given on page 95.

Walkers and the Law

The Countryside and Rights of Way Act (CRoW Act 2000) extends the rights of access previously enjoyed by walkers in England and Wales. Implementation of these rights began on 19 September 2004. The Act amends existing legislation and for the first time provides access on foot to certain types of land – defined as mountain, moor, heath, down and registered common land.

Where You Can Go

Rights of Way

Prior to the introduction of the CRoW Act, walkers could only legally access the countryside along public rights of way. These are either 'footpaths' (for walkers only) or 'bridleways' (for walkers, riders on horseback and pedal cyclists). A third category called 'Byways open to all traffic' (BOATs), is used by motorised vehicles as well as those using non-mechanised transport. Mainly they are green lanes, farm and estate roads, although occasionally they will be found crossing mountainous areas.

Rights of way are marked on Ordnance Survey maps. Look for the green broken lines on the Explorer maps, or the red dashed lines on Landranger maps.

The term 'right of way' means exactly what it says. It gives a right of passage over what, for the most part, is private land. Under pre-CRoW legislation walkers were required to keep to the line of the right of way and not stray onto land on either side. If you did inadvertently wander off the right of way, either because of faulty map reading or because the route was not clearly indicated on the ground, you were technically trespassing.

Local authorities have a legal obligation to ensure that rights of way are kept clear and free of obstruction, and are signposted where they leave metalled roads. The duty of local authorities to install signposts extends to the placing of signs along a path or way, but only where the authority considers it necessary to have a signpost or waymark to assist persons unfamiliar with the locality.

The New Access Rights
Access Land
As well as being able to walk on existing rights of way, under the new legislation you now have access to large areas of open land. You can of course continue to use rights of way footpaths to cross this land, but the main difference is that you can now lawfully leave the path and wander at will, but only in areas designated as access land.

Where to Walk
Areas now covered by the new access rights – Access Land – are shown on Ordnance Survey Explorer maps bearing the access land symbol on the front cover.

'Access Land' is shown on Ordnance Survey maps by a light yellow tint surrounded by a pale orange border. New orange coloured 'i' symbols on the maps will show the location of permanent access information boards installed by the access authorities.

Restrictions
The right to walk on access land may lawfully be restricted by landowners. Landowners can, for any reason, restrict access for up to 28 days in any year. They cannot however close the land:
• on bank holidays;
• for more than four Saturdays and Sundays in a year;
• on any Saturday from 1 June to 11 August; or
• on any Sunday from 1 June to the end of September.
They have to provide local authorities with five working days' notice before the date of closure unless the land involved is an area of less than five hectares or the closure is for less than four hours. In these cases landowners only need to provide two hours' notice.

Whatever restrictions are put into place on access land they have no effect on existing rights of way, and you can continue to walk on them.

Dogs
Dogs can be taken on access land, but must be kept on leads of two metres or less between 1 March and 31 July, and at all times where they are near livestock. In addition landowners may impose a ban on all dogs from fields where lambing takes place for up to six weeks in any year. Dogs may be banned from moorland used for grouse shooting and breeding for up to five years.

In the main, walkers following the routes in this book will continue to follow existing rights of way, but a knowledge and understanding of the law as it affects walkers, plus the ability to distinguish access land marked on the maps, will enable anyone who wishes to depart from paths that cross access land either to take a shortcut, to enjoy a view or to explore.

General Obstructions
Obstructions can sometimes cause a problem on a walk and the most common of these is where the path across a field has been ploughed over. It is legal for a farmer to plough up a path provided that it is restored within two weeks. This does not always happen and you are faced with the dilemma of following the line of the path, even if this means treading on crops, or walking round the edge of the field. Although the later course of action seems the most sensible, it does mean that you would be trespassing.

Other obstructions can vary from overhanging vegetation to wire fences across the path, locked gates or even a cattle feeder on the path.

Use common sense. If you can get round the obstruction without causing damage, do so. Otherwise only remove as much of the obstruction as is necessary to secure passage.

If the right of way is blocked and cannot be followed, there is a long-standing view that in such circumstances there is a right to deviate, but this cannot wholly be relied on. Although it is accepted in law that highways (and that includes rights of way) are for the public service, and if the usual track is impassable, it is for the general

Countryside Access Charter

Your rights of way arc:

- public footpaths – on foot only. Sometimes waymarked in yellow
- bridleways – on foot, horseback and pedal cycle. Sometimes waymarked in blue
- byways (usually old roads), most 'roads used as public paths' and, of course, public roads – all traffic has the right of way

Use maps, signs and waymarks to check rights of way. Ordnance Survey Explorer and Landranger maps show most public rights of way

On rights of way you can:

- take a pram, pushchair or wheelchair if practicable
- take a dog (on a lead or under close control)
- take a short route round an illegal obstruction or remove it sufficiently to get past

You have a right to go for recreation to:

- public parks and open spaces – on foot
- most commons near older towns and cities – on foot and sometimes on horseback
- private land where the owner has a formal agreement with the local authority

In addition you can use the following by local or established custom or consent, but ask for advice if you are unsure:

- many areas of open country, such as moorland, fell and coastal areas, especially those in the care of the National Trust, and some commons
- some woods and forests, especially those owned by the Forestry Commission
- country parks and picnic sites
- most beaches
- canal towpaths
- some private paths and tracks Consent sometimes extends to horse-riding and cycling

For your information:

- county councils and London boroughs maintain and record rights of way, and register commons
- obstructions, dangerous animals, harassment and misleading signs on rights of way are illegal and you should report them to the county council
- paths across fields can be ploughed, but must normally be reinstated within two weeks
- landowners can require you to leave land to which you have no right of access
- motor vehicles are normally permitted only on roads, byways and some 'roads used as public paths'

Further Information

---

good that people should be entitled to pass into another line. However, this should not be taken as indicating a right to deviate whenever a way becomes impassable. If in doubt, retreat.

Report obstructions to the local authority and/or the Ramblers' Association.

Global Positioning System (GPS)

What is GPS?

GPS is a worldwide radio navigation system that uses a network of 24 satellites and receivers, usually hand-held, to calculate positions. By measuring the time it takes a signal to reach the receiver, the distance from the satellite can be estimated. Repeat this with several satellites and the receiver can then use triangulation to establish the position of the receiver.

How to use GPS with Ordnance Survey mapping

Each of the walks in this book includes GPS co-ordinate data that reflects the walk position points on Ordnance Survey maps.

GPS and OS maps use different models for the earth and co-ordinate systems, so when you are trying to relate your GPS position to features on the map the two will differ slightly. This is especially the case with height, as the model that relates the GPS global co-ordinate system to height above sea level is very poor.

When using GPS with OS mapping,

some distortion – up to 16ft (5m) – will always be present. Moreover, individual features on maps may have been surveyed only to an accuracy of 23ft (7m) (for 1:25000 scale maps), while other features, e.g. boulders, are usually only shown schematically.

In practice, this should not cause undue difficulty, as you will be near enough to your objective to be able to spot it.

How to use the GPS data in this book
There are various ways you can use the GPS data in this book.

1. Follow the route description while checking your position on your receiver when you are approaching a position point.

2. You can also use the positioning information on your receiver to verify where you are on the map.

3. Alternatively, you can use some of the proprietary software that is available. At the simple end there is inexpensive software, which lets you input the walk positions (waypoints), download them to the gps unit and then use them to assist your navigation on the walks.

At the upper end of the market Ordnance Survey maps are available in electronic form. Most come with software that enables you to enter your walking route onto the map, download it to your gps unit and use it, alongside the route description, to follow the route.

Safety on the Hills

The hills, mountains and moorlands of Britain, though of modest height compared with those in many other countries, need to be treated with respect. Friendly and inviting in good weather, they can quickly be transformed into wet, misty, windswept and potentially dangerous areas of wilderness in bad weather. Even on an outwardly fine and settled summer day, conditions can rapidly deteriorate at high altitudes and, in winter, even more so.

Therefore it is advisable to always take both warm and waterproof clothing, sufficient nourishing food, a hot drink, first-aid kit, torch and whistle. Wear suitable footwear, such as strong walking boots or shoes that give a good grip over rocky terrain and on slippery slopes. Try to obtain a local weather forecast and bear it in mind before you start. Do not be afraid to abandon your proposed route and return to your starting point in the event of a sudden and unexpected deterioration in the weather. Do not go alone and allow enough time to finish the walk well before nightfall.

Most of the walks described in this book do not venture into remote wilderness areas and will be safe to do, given due care and respect, at any time of year in all but the most unreasonable weather. Indeed, a crisp, fine winter day often provides perfect walking conditions, with firm ground underfoot and a clarity that is not possible to achieve in the other seasons of the year. A few walks, however, are suitable only for reasonably fit and experienced hill walkers able to use a compass and should definitely not be tackled by anyone else during the winter months or in bad weather, especially high winds and mist. These are indicated in the general description that precedes each of the walks.

Useful Organisations

Campaign to Protect Rural England
128 Southwark Street, London SE1 0SW
Tel. 020 7981 2800
www.cpre.org.uk

Council for National Parks
6-7 Barnard Mews, London SW11 1QU
Tel. 020 7924 4077
www.cnp.org.uk

Dartmoor National Park Authority
Parke, Bovey Tracey,
Newton Abbot TQ13 9JQ
Tel. 01626 832093
www.dartmoor-npa.gov.uk
See also: www.virtuallydartmoor.org.uk
National Park visitor centres:
Haytor: 01364 661520

Further Information

Newbridge: 01364 631303
Postbridge: 01822 880272
Princetown, High Moorland Visitor
Centre: 01822 890414
Local DNPA information points:
Belstone, The Tors (Pub)
Chagford, Courtyard Café
Christow post office
Drewsteignton post office
Horrabridge, Summerfield newsagent
Lydford petrol station
Meavy, The Royal Oak Inn
Sticklepath, Sticklepath Post Office
Widecombe, Sexton's Cottage (NT shop)
Yelverton petrol station

Forestry Commission England
Great Eastern House, Tenison Road,
Cambridge CB1 2DU
Tel. 01223 314546
www.forestry.gov.uk

Long Distance Walkers' Association
www.ldwa.org.uk

National Trust
Membership and general enquiries:
PO Box 39, Warrington WA5 7WD
Tel. 0870 458 4000
www.nationaltrust.org.uk
Devon Regional Office:
Killerton House, Broadclyst, Exeter EX5 3LE
Tel. 01392 881691

Natural England
1 East Parade, Sheffield S1 2ET
Tel. 0114 241 8920
www.naturalengland.org.uk

Ordnance Survey
Romsey Road, Southampton SO16 4GU
Tel. 08456 05 05 05
www.ordnancesurvey.co.uk

Ramblers' Association
2nd Floor, Camelford House, 87–90 Albert
Embankment, London SE1 7TW
Tel. 020 7339 8500
www.ramblers.org.uk

Tourist information
Dartmoor Tourist Association
High Moorland Business Centre,
Princetown PL20 6QF
Tel. 01822 890567
www.discoverdartmoor.co.uk

South West Tourism
Woodwater Park, Exeter
EX2 5WT
Tel. 01392 360050
www.swtourism.co.uk

Tourist information centres:
Okehampton: 01837 53020
www.okehamptondevon.co.uk
Tavistock: 01822 612938
www.tavistock-devon.co.uk
Community information centres:
Ashburton: 01364 653426
www.ashburton.org
Bovey Tracey: 01626 832047
www.boveytracey.gov.uk
Buckfastleigh: 01364 644522
www.buckfastleigh.org
Ivybridge: 01752 897035
Moretonhampstead: 01647 440043

Youth Hostels Association
Trevelyan House, Dimple Road,
Matlock DE4 3YH
Tel. 0870 770 8868
www.yha.org.uk

 ## Ordnance Survey Maps of Dartmoor

Dartmoor is covered by Ordnance Survey
1:50 000 scale (2cm to 1km or 1¼ inches
to 1 mile) Landranger map sheets 191, 192,
201 and 202. These all-purpose maps are
packed with information to help you explore
the area. Viewpoints, picnic sites, places of
interest and caravan and camping sites are
shown, as well as public rights of way information such as footpaths and bridleways.

To examine Dartmoor in more detail,
and especially if you are planning walks,
Ordnance Survey Explorer maps OL28
(Dartmoor) and 110 (Torquay & Dawlish)
both at 1:25 000 scale (4cm to 1km or
2½ inches to 1 mile) are ideal.

To get to Dartmoor, use the Ordnance
Survey OS Travel Map-Route Great Britain
at 1:625 000 scale (4cm to 25km or 1 inch
to 10 miles) or Ordnance Survey OS Travel
Map Road (South West England & South
Wales).

Ordnance Survey maps and guides are
available from most booksellers, stationers
and newsagents.

www.totalwalking.co.uk

www.totalwalking.co.uk
is the official website of the Jarrold
Pathfinder and Short Walks guides. This
interactive website features a wealth of
information for walkers – from the latest
news on route diversions and advice from
professional walkers to product news, free
sample walks and promotional offers.